KT-214-471

NORTH KOREA

GOOD NEWS REACHES
THE HERMIT KINGDOM

The **Voice**
of the **Martyrs**

with P. Todd Nettleton

Living Sacrifice Book Company
Bartlesville, OK 74005

**North Korea: Good News Reaches the
Hermit Kingdom**

Living Sacrifice Book Company
P.O. Box 2273
Bartlesville, OK 74005-2273

ISBN 978-0-88264-030-3

Edited by Lynn Copeland

Cover by Lookout Design

Page design and layout by Genesis Group

Printed in the United States of America

Unless otherwise indicated, Scripture references are from the Holman Christian Standard Bible, © 1999, 2000, 2002, 2003 by Holman Bible Publishers, Nashville Tennessee.

"So we called out to the LORD, the God of our fathers, and the LORD heard our cry and saw our misery, hardship, and oppression."

—DEUTERONOMY 26:7

*"North Korean children should not
starve while a massive army is fed.
No nation should be a prison for
its own people."*

—PRESIDENT GEORGE W. BUSH,
February 2002

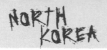

CONTENTS

ACKNOWLEDGMENTS

This book would have been impossible without information and encouragement from many people. Those who are intimately involved in Christian ministry in North Korea cannot be named here because to do so would put their lives at risk. God knows their names, though, and the honor their lives and ministries are bringing to Him. Their reward will be great in heaven.

I am particularly grateful for the unpublished graduate research material provided by Bahnseok Lee of Cornerstone Ministries. His research provided a great foundation for my writing and for my understanding of the church in North Korea.

The leadership at The Voice of the Martyrs, especially Executive Director Tom White, has seen the need for small books such as this to inform the Church and invite them to take action on behalf of Christians who suffer for their faith. VOM's resource committee has been vital in that process and very supportive of this project.

Steve Cleary has a passion for the Christians of North Korea and for telling the world their stories; his insights have driven this project forward, and his passion has ensured these words would have maximum effect on their behalf.

My parents lived out their commitment to Christ, even crossing the sea to follow His call. My first brush with heroic faith stories was in the missionary books my dad read to my brother and me. Mom and Dad trained me well, and I am thankful.

My sons, Kameron and Kedrick, sacrificed a lot of "dad time" to the completion of this project. May they both grow in faith and commitment to Christ from knowing these stories, and may they walk as today's heroes of the faith in North Korea are walking.

My wife, Charlotte, sacrificed many hours with me so that I could complete this project. At times she couldn't bear to read the stories of suffering and persecution it contains, but she encouraged my efforts to tell those stories. Working at VOM is not "my" ministry; it is ours. I could not do it effectively without her love and support.

Finally, I honor my Korean brothers and sisters who are willing to die rather than deny their Savior. Their courage inspires me. Their testimonies instruct me. Their faithfulness leaves me in awe.

Lord, may I also be faithful to You.

P. TODD NETTLETON

INTRODUCTION:
THE BRIEF MISSIONARY CAREER OF ROBERT THOMAS

Robert J. Thomas must have felt like a pioneer as he boarded the ship. His meager possessions occupied only a small corner of his travel chest. The rest was filled with five hundred Chinese Bibles. The leather straps and brass buckles on the case strained to hold the heavy load. Thomas earned his passage by offering to translate for the ship's captain when they arrived in Korea. His real purpose was to carry the gospel of Jesus Christ into the Hermit Kingdom. He knew it was dangerous. Only a few years earlier, the Korean government had rounded up more than eight thousand Catholics and slaughtered them. Thomas' first contact with Korean people was with two Koreans who had fled this persecution and escaped to China.

Thomas was a Welsh missionary to China, but his heart's desire was to carry Christ's message to Korea. His sacrifice for God's Kingdom was already great: Four months after arriving in China in 1863, he buried his wife. In 1865, he had made his first trip to Korea, a two-month visit to Chang-Lin Island. He'd handed out Chinese gospel tracts and tried to learn as much as he could about the people and their language. His broken heart continued to burn for the lost souls of Korea. His passion was to bring the gospel to them.

He saw a chance to return the following year when he learned that an American ship, the *General Sherman*, was planning to sail right up the Dae-dong River into Pyongyang. Their goal was to survey the land and establish trading relations with the Hermit Kingdom, which to that point had been completely closed to foreigners.

Thomas went to the ship's captain, telling of his previous experience in Korea and offering his services as translator if he could share the gospel once they arrived in Korea. The nation was such an unknown land, with so few foreign visitors that the captain thought having someone along who had been there before (and returned alive) couldn't hurt, so he agreed to take Thomas along.

Thomas was thrilled, believing this open door was a God-ordained appointment for him to carry the gospel to the Korean people.

Thomas brought his chest aboard. Soon they set sail, first into the Yellow Sea, then into the mouth of the Dae-dong River. But the Koreans with whom they hoped to open relations were not welcoming. The ship, a converted Navy gunship, was denied permission to anchor, and the crew was denied trading privileges.

Thomas tried to reason with the government messengers, repeatedly telling them that the ship's mission was peaceful, that they simply wanted to open relations and trade for goods. Thomas tried to remain calm as he explained, again and again, their purpose. He kept repeating the Korean word for peace, over and over, trying to keep his voice calm and reasonable, trying to appease the hostile officials, praying silently for wisdom with each word.

Each time the government messengers left the boat, Thomas tried just as hard to communicate clearly with the captain their fear and mistrust of the outsiders. He understood very clearly the word they kept repeating as they pointed back down the river, the way the *General Sherman* had come: *dduhnara* ("leave, go away").

Perhaps we should go now and try again later, Thomas may have suggested to the captain. *If they see us leave peacefully, they may understand that we mean them no harm. Perhaps we could sail back to the mouth of the river and anchor there and continue to negotiate.* Thomas's passion was to land his feet on Korean soil and begin to share the gospel. The possibility of violence and of unsaved Koreans dying must have pained him greatly.

The American captain wouldn't take no for an answer. The orders he'd been given were clear: Open the port and the country for trade. His initial courtesy and deference were fading into anger and hostility. His options shrunk considerably when the *General Sherman* ran aground on a sand bar and stuck fast. Robert Thomas was left to translate as the captain and crew tried to negotiate a way out.

Negotiations quickly broke down as the Koreans realized the ship was stranded. Thomas's repeated use of the Korean word for peace fell on deaf ears.

Angry Koreans on shore threw stones and flaming pieces of wood toward the ship. The Americans answered with random gunfire to try to scare the Koreans away. Some historians believe as many as twenty Koreans were killed by the shots.

For two weeks the ship remained grounded. Thomas tossed Bibles to the shore and desperately tried to talk the Koreans toward a peaceful resolution. He prayed that God would help them find a way out, and that God would help him speak and understand the Korean language clearly. But his peace-making efforts were beaten out by the random gunfire and the senseless spilling of Korean blood.

Finally, the Koreans loaded a boat with pine branches and lit them on fire, then sent it downriver toward the *General Sherman*. Their plan worked, and soon the American ship was engulfed in flames.

Even as the fire raged around him, Robert Thomas did not waver from his mission. He threw the Bibles toward shore, shouting the name of Jesus and peaceful sayings in Korean, a witness for Christ even as the flames rose.

With their burning ship beginning to sink, the American crew was forced to jump into the river and attempt to flee. They were slaughtered as they reached the shore.

Missionary Robert Thomas came to shore carrying one of the red-covered Bibles, offering it to the man who ran toward him. Thomas said, "Jesus, Jesus," in Korean, holding the book out toward the man. Then he knelt to pray.

Thomas never said "amen" to that prayer. Some accounts tell of a mighty swing of a machete that cut off the Welshman's head, which was then picked up and tossed into the muddy water. Other accounts of that day's events say a primitive spear went right through Thomas's heart. One thing is clear: Thomas's life ended only minutes after his feet touched the sandy Korean shore.

It was a sad end to a committed missionary life. What a waste, some might say, for a twenty-six-year-old man to die only a few moments after setting foot in the nation God had called him to.

But in God's Kingdom there are no wasted moments. The martyrs' blood is too precious.

The Korean who killed Robert Thomas, a man named Park, was convicted in his spirit. He came to believe he had taken the life of a good man. He picked up the red-covered Book and took it home. He tore out the pages and carefully used them to wallpaper his guesthouse. Later, after reading the words, Park chose to follow Christ.

Years later, when an American missionary came to the area, he asked Park about the unique decorations.

"Oh, yes," he was told, "many people have come from all over Korea to read my walls." The man who had taken the life of Robert Thomas ended up sharing Life with many others. His family continued to carry on Thomas's gospel legacy.

Park's nephew went on to attend Bible College in Pyongyang, and later served as a part of the team updating the Korean Bible translation, modernizing the words that he'd first read on the walls of his uncle's guesthouse.

The North Korean government has their own version of the demise of the *General Sherman*. Their history books claim it was Kim Ung-u, the great grandfather of dictator Kim Il Sung, who lit the ship on fire. This propaganda is used to show the "Dear Leader's" family has always been at the forefront of the battle to keep "imperialists" out of Korea.

Early church historian Tertullian said, "The blood of the martyrs is the seed of the church." Robert Thomas's blood, shed on a river bank, and the blood of many others—Korean Christians and foreign missionaries who also laid down their lives—grew into a church that still exists in North Korea. This cycle of suffering that has been repeated countless times in the Hermit Kingdom continues today.

Today thousands of North Korean Christians are imprisoned in *kwanliso*, "special control institutions"—political prisoner camps. These camps, run by the Ministry of State Security's seventh bureau, are reserved for political prisoners and their families. It is unknown exactly how many people are in the camps or how many die in them each year, but it is known that many Christians are among them. Satellite photos show sprawling compounds, sometimes 20 miles long and 10 miles wide and containing multiple "villages," each surrounded by high walls, watch towers, and razor wire. Scholars estimate that at least a million Koreans have died in such camps. The beating and killing of prisoners by the guards is not only tolerated in such camps, but encouraged. In 1968, Kim Il Sung instructed guards in such camps "not to feel the slightest humanity or empathy for class enemies."

The average life expectancy for a prisoner in the *kwanliso* is only five years. For a person convicted of worshiping "the God of heaven" (the North Korean government's derogatory term for the deity believed by His followers to have created the heavens and the earth), the average prison sentence is fifteen years. Yet Koreans willingly embrace Christ's gospel. As one writer put it, "As long as there have been Korean Christians, there have been Koreans ready to die for their faith."

Just as Robert Thomas's sacrifice resulted in Christian believers, the sacrifice of Christians today in North Korea is producing a harvest of souls and a vibrant church. This book shares a brief overview of North Korea's rich spiritual heritage and what the steadfast faith of believers costs them—yesterday and today—as they follow Christ at the mercy of a ruthless dictator.

A PENCIL IN THE
HANDS OF THE MASTER

When the Christian worker in Northern China had four young men knock on his door a few years ago, he knew he had to help them. "Paul" (all names in this article have been changed for their protection) was working with North Koreans who had crossed the border, helping them find food and sharing with them the love of Christ.

Paul encouraged the four to choose fake names, since their presence in China and in his home was illegal, so that even if their conversations were overheard and reported, the police wouldn't know their real names. The youngsters were too creative to choose the Korean equivalents of Bob, John, Jim, or Mike; instead they became known as Pencil, Eraser, Pen, and Paper Clip. The names were suggested by the one who became Pencil; he seemed an undisciplined, out-of-control kid who refused to grow up.

Paul shared the gospel with them and all four committed their lives to Christ. As he began to disciple the boys, he thought three of them had real potential to carry the gospel back into their homeland. But Pencil seemed unlikely to do anything worthwhile. He never paid attention. When Paul was trying to teach, Pencil was sketching on a paper or staring off into space. The other three loved their friend and the spontaneity he brought to the group. To Paul, though, Pencil was an irri-

tant. He wondered if any good would ever come in the young man's life.

After several months of discipleship, the missionary felt ready to send the young men back into North Korea. But he didn't send Pencil; he simply felt that the boy wasn't ready or interested in such a mission.

Even though Paul hadn't included Pencil, the other three weren't going anywhere without their friend. Together the four crossed back into North Korea. Before they left, Paul told them, "No matter what you do, or what trouble you're in, you can come back here and I'll try to help you." Months passed without any report of the group. Paul wondered if they had safely crossed the river or been caught by the soldiers that constantly patrol with orders to shoot on sight.

Six months after crossing, three of the four were arrested by State Security police. Pencil watched frozen in fear as his friends were beaten by the police and arrested for sharing Christ with others. As soon as the vehicles carrying his three friends were out of sight, he ran. He later heard that they'd been taken to a concentration camp, but he never saw them again.

Pencil was too afraid to go to anyone he knew, for fear that the police were looking for him. Instead of going back to his relatives, Pencil became a beggar.

As he thought of his friends, he marveled at how they had shared the gospel. At any opportunity they would speak of Christ and how He had brought hope into their lives even as they lived in hopeless surroundings. But Pencil never seemed able to share his faith. His mouth became dry, his hands shook, and he couldn't get the words out. Sometimes other beggars, seeing the hope in his eyes, would open the door to a conversation about Jesus Christ by saying, "You look different. You don't even look like a North Korean." But even then Pencil was unable to tell them that the difference came from inside of him, where Christ lived.

One day Pencil remembered Paul's words: "You can come back here and I'll try to help you." But would he? Pencil had spent most of his time there ignoring the Christian's words. He decided to cross the river again into China and seek out Paul, to see if he really would help him—or if he'd even remember him.

It had been eight months since the four young men crossed the Tumen; now only one was left to retrace their steps.

With tears in his eyes, Pencil told the Christian worker the fate of his three friends. He shared how they had been bold witnesses for Christ, while he had cowered and hidden in fear as his best friends were being bound and taken away.

"What do you want to do with the rest of your life?" Paul asked the young man.

"I want to learn how to be brave like my friends, and unafraid to share Jesus."

The Christian worker who had written off the young man and assumed that no good fruit would ever show in his life now put aside that judgment and spent two months of intense discipleship, investing each day into Pencil's life. He could see the young man's faith growing and his commitment deepening as they studied the Scriptures and prayed together. "What more do you need?" Paul asked when it seemed that Pencil was ready to cross once again into his home country.

The boy whose mind always seemed to wander now looked directly into the eyes of his friend and mentor. "I need nothing more."

Paul helped Pencil connect with a Christian couple inside North Korea, and the three of them began a ministry to homeless people. There were thousands of hurting, hungry people in need of hope. The couple taught Pencil how to strike up conversations with them, and then how to steer the discussion into matters of Spirit and eternity. Pencil found himself sharing the gospel story with the poorest of the poor.

"Where did you get this mysterious story?" some asked. One beggar came up to Pencil and confided that he was a Christian also. Others asked him to tell more of the story, or to start at the beginning and tell it again. For five months the ministry continued, planting seeds and then watering, praying and watering again.

One day the three of them shared with a group of beggars. With some they left tracts and with one they shared a Bible. The young beggar went home and proudly showed the book to his mother, telling her about the kind people who had given it to him.

The mother knew that this was a religious book, and that as such it had to be illegal. Was someone trying to frame her son? Would the whole family be arrested? She grabbed the book and headed to the police station. They listened to her story, then questioned her son. Finally they took him to where he said he'd gotten the book. Pencil was still there, and the boy identified him to police as the one who'd given him the contraband book. Pencil was arrested. The couple he was working with were followed and watched, then also taken into custody.

At the police station, the questions quickly turned to interrogation, and then to torture. The police demanded to know where Pencil had gotten the Bible. They offered to let him walk out the door if he would renounce Jesus. Pencil steadfastly refused their offer.

"I have surrendered my life to Jesus," he told them. "I cannot deny Him."

Rather than reveal the source of the Bible, he told the police about Pen, Eraser, and Paper Clip. He spoke of their witness for Christ, and the fearless way they followed Him.

"There was a time when I couldn't be like them," he said. "I was too afraid. But now I can be since Jesus is with me."

Wanting to break the teen-ager, and angry and insulted by his lack of fear, the police beat him. The beating didn't change his stand for Christ.

"We are big sinners here in North Korea because we do not believe in God," Pencil told them. "Even if you kill me, someday you will see the truth I stand for and you too will become a Christian."

That prophecy made the police even more enraged. One by one, they pulled out Pencil's fingernails. Barely alive, the young man was sent to a political prisoner camp. It was a labor camp, but in an effort to break his spirit orders were given that Pencil be allowed no food, yet his labor quota remained the same.

Pencil never focused on his hunger or hardship, though. Each day he told the other prisoners, and even the guards, "Jesus is the reason I am able to go on." Because of his endurance without food and his willingness to continue to share the love of Jesus, many in the camp turned to Christ.

After two months in the camp, Pencil died. He never saw his twentieth birthday. His body was removed from the camp, but the fruit of his short ministry there lived on.

Shortly after his death, the Christian couple who had ministered with Pencil were sent to that same camp. When they arrived they were surprised to find Christians there—Christians who told them of the death of their friend and co-worker.

They had been there only a few days when the camp's top State Security Agency officer ordered them brought to his office. He told them that he had been troubled by Pencil's death. He knew that they had been associated with the young man, and told them that he was going to release them.

A few days later, the couple was surprised to find the same officer knocking on the door of their home. He wanted to talk to them further.

"I have tortured and killed many people," he told them, "but since the death of this young man I have been troubled." He told them the story of their friend's courage and cheerful spirit, even as his body was failing.

"Pencil" and the woman on the left paid with their lives for being Christians in North Korea.

When the official had finished, the couple told him that he needed to get down on his knees while they told him why Pencil was different. They told him about Jesus, who lived inside of Pencil and gave him courage, peace, and strength, and he surrendered his life to Christ. When they finished sharing and praying together, the agent invited them to come with him.

They followed him to his large home. Inside were gathered eight of his family members, as well as several soldiers who worked at the camp, along with their families. They listened intently as the young couple spoke of Jesus' love, His death on the cross for their sins, and the gospel plan of salvation. Many of the listeners wept quietly.

When the couple was finished, the official was shocked as his own mother stepped forward and said that for fifty years she had been a secret Christian.

"I am no longer ashamed of my faith," she explained, then she said to the couple, "I want you to pray for me and I want to give a tithe to Jesus."

She then turned to the rest of the people gathered in the room. "Who wants to surrender their life to Jesus?" she asked.

Everyone in the room raised their hand. Each of them was baptized that night.

"I was not kind to Pencil because I did not think he would amount to much," Paul says softly now. Yet this young man's witness and courage brought many to Christ.

NORTH KOREA TODAY

A Testimony

The following letter was written by a Korean Christian worker. The letter was given to VOM workers in the summer of 2005.

I give all glory to my Lord, to the One who picked me up and rescued my soul from eternal death.

I went into North Korea early in 2004, to meet with some appointed families. They were living in such terrible conditions that I could not look at them without tears. I bought some clothing for them, as it was bitter cold.

I was then to travel to another village to meet with a family that was referred to me by a woman in our church named Ms. Park. Ms. Park also gave me her cousin's identification papers to help protect my identity. But on my way to the village I was stopped by the police, and when they saw the ID she had given me, I was immediately arrested. I thought I could trust Ms. Park, but she is obviously a North Korean spy.

For fourteen days I was interrogated daily. Because of the beatings I received, I began to have severe pains in my liver and kidney. My whole body shook uncontrollably. When I tried to stand, I collapsed on the floor. They took all my money and hired two guards who were experts in judo to torture me.

Fearing I would die, officials transferred me to another location and fed me well until I regained my strength. They told me, "You shouldn't die yet."

In two weeks I had recovered so they brought me back to the interrogation center where I was again beaten and tortured for another fifty-four days. During this time, I would think of Joseph, who also spent time in prison, and Daniel in the lion's den. God was unchanged; as He was with those before me, He would watch over me. I kept my faith.

My number one "crime" against the Democratic People's Republic of Korea is that for the past eight years, I have been spreading the gospel in North Korea (NK), bringing people to Christ. My number two crime is that I've been teaching the NK refugee kids about Christianity, planting "seeds of destruction." My number three crime is having worked with Korean-Americans.

I've been absurdly accused of partnering with spies from America. They have convicted me of "partaking in the destruction of our great leader's regime in Korea" as well as for "building God's Kingdom" in NK. They've accused me of threatening the political system as well as the power of the regime. With all the crimes above and more, they've decided to keep me in the prison camps. After all, to them, I didn't even deserve to live.

The prison camps are like a living hell. A man I saw had been arrested for stealing. They beat him so badly that he became mentally unstable. Once in a while, he'd say, "Just kill me!" Because of this, the guards kicked him and stepped on him until he was half-dead. Then they released him temporarily and arrested him again. They beat him every morning with thick bats because he wasn't able to walk properly. He became unrecognizable. He started developing a bloody pus all over, along with severe diarrhea. When he couldn't control his diarrhea, they would beat him and confiscate his meals—a few spoonfuls of rice. He got so hungry he started to eat dirty rags that were used to clean the toilets. He spent twenty-eight days in the prison. Not a soul who was there consoled him, and just like that he died in his prison cell. What a tragedy...This is the reality of North Korean prison camps. When I think about it, I cannot help crying.

This man was not the only one being beaten and tortured in these prison camps. Once the prison guards notice you, or even if they just want to beat somebody, they will torture you. Who you are is not important to them. You can be an old grandma or a grandpa—it doesn't matter. They swear at you and beat you relentlessly. I've seen it all. It is said that half of the prisoners in the interrogation center will die within ten months.

Many prisoners were people who had tried to escape to China. One man was only seeking to get medicine for his sick son. He'd been in the camp for ten months. He was thirty years old, but because he was so skinny, I thought he was an old man in his seventies. One time when he was changing his shirt, his skeletal frame was revealed. This enraged all the prisoners because it showed the brutality of the prison camps.

Among the defectors, the oldest man was seventy-eight years old. The youngest was nine years old—an orphan who had wandered out in search of food and ended up living in China for a few months before getting caught.

I have some heroes of faith that I look up to. When I was in the prison camp, my spot was right next to the cell leader. He found out I was imprisoned for evangelizing in NK. By this time, everyone knew I was a Christian. Since I had a good relationship with him, I had the opportunity to explain the existence of God and of Christ. He confessed to me that in 1999, he killed not just one but two missionaries caught evangelizing in North Korea. It was clear that he was deeply regretting his actions. He shared that the two missionaries had kept their faith to the very end, even to the point of death. They are my heroes of faith. They died alone, in a foreign land, away from their loved ones. When I think about them, my heart aches, but I know God rewards these martyrs with greater treasures.

While these people are shivering in their cold cells, there are others in their warm rooms. While there are people who cry out to God, "Lord, I'm hungry," there are others who are full, never having known hunger. While there are people shedding tears of pain as they are relentlessly beaten, there are others who sing hymns and praises freely. I honor these martyrs' labor. They truly live and die for the gospel, and they are my heroes. Though their lives were short, what they've done will forever shine with Christ.

Another prisoner was a twenty-five-year-old Christian who had brought a Bible from China back into North Korea. She got caught crossing the Tumen River. She had already been in the camps nearly a year of her three-year sentence. Another Christian woman of nineteen was caught with four Bibles. She has since disappeared.

I was so sad when a Christian was transferred out of our prison to the execution camp. He was only a teenager.

I know the cries of North Koreans as they're beaten. I know their tears of hunger...moaning in pain that doesn't end. I know their dark faces with no smiles. I picture these faces. I picture the shadows of hell (prison camps, execution camps, forced labor, re-education), and many of these North Koreans die without knowing our Lord who gives eternal life. I know the tears they've shed. I hear their pitiful moans. I believe we, as Christians, need to know these are the cries and the moans of their souls pleading to know the way to Life, away from the eternal fire of hell.

In Christ,
"Mr. Lee"

P.S. The North Korean government threatened me at our every encounter that if I disclosed anything I saw or heard to anyone, they would hire their people in China to kill me and all my family.

Concerning my release, the officers told me that if I stole two cars for them, they would let me go. I refused and told them that I would die in prison before stealing for them. Then they offered to let me go for U.S. $10,000. We finally agreed upon 30,000 *won*. I want to thank those who paid my debt.[1] If I had chosen to give up my life in NK, they could have saved that money. I'm sorry for spending that money and coming back alive.

I'm thankful for His grace that protects my life and grants me the opportunity to share the love that my Lord Jesus Christ demonstrated on the cross. It is truly more precious than my own life.

---

1 VOM paid our brother's fine through our Families of Martyrs Fund.

THE FIRST CHRISTIANS IN
THE HERMIT KINGDOM

Though Robert Thomas is known today as the first Western martyr in Korea, he was not the first Christian to minister on Korean soil. Korea's earliest encounters with Christianity either were not recorded or were lost. Given the severity of persecution and the many intrusions by foreign powers in the last few centuries, it is understandable that suspicious materials possibly costing a person his or her life were destroyed.

There isn't enough clear documentation to say with certainty when Korea's first encounter with Christianity occurred. A few records, and some circumstantial evidence, allow the possibility that the Shilla Dynasty (57 B.C. to A.D. 935) may have encountered the story of Christ through contact with Nestorians during the T'ang Dynasty of China, in the seventh century. Another probable route for the Shilla to have come across Nestorian teachings about Christ was in documents from Arabs in the ninth century. The first documented Korean Christians would come much later.

Jesuit Priests and Japanese Prisoners
Hideyoshi, sometimes called "the Japanese Napoleon," invaded Korea in 1592. When he was done ravaging the country, the destruction was so complete "not even earthworms could live."

One missionary to Japan at that time wrote that three hundred of the prisoners from "Corai" (Korea) had converted to Christianity. Less than twenty years later, there were ordained Korean priests serving in Japan. The Jesuit leaders had in mind to use these men to spread the gospel back to Korea. But those plans died with the men who held them during the bloody persecutions that began in Japan in 1614.

It would be another two hundred years before the gospel message reached the Koreans in their homeland. When it finally arrived, it came from China rather than Japan. During those two centuries, Korean travelers and diplomats carried into the country different Christian books, including Matthew Ricci's *True Doctrine of the Lord of Heaven*. But the books were mostly ignored.

Beginning about 1777, however, Korean scholars rediscovered the books and began to study them to put their teachings into practice. In 1783, the scholars sent a representative to Peking (now Beijing) to consult with the Jesuits there about their teachings, so they could return with more information. The man they sent, Sung-Heun Lee, went even further than research: He converted to Christianity and was baptized, taking on the Christian name Peter Lee. He returned to Korea in 1784, bringing books, crosses, and the Christian faith with him.

The period following Lee's return is sometimes called "the century of Roman Catholic missions."

The century saw the growth of Christianity, and with it the first government edict against the new faith, as Korea was still considered the Hermit Kingdom and didn't welcome foreign teaching.

In the following decade, more than four hundred Korean Christians were publicly martyred as Korea's leaders fought against this new, "foreign" religion.

The first foreign missionary arrived at the end of that decade, a priest from China named James Chu. After six months of open ministry, Chu was forced to go into hiding. He hid from the authorities for three years, after which the government issued a public proclamation outlawing the young priest. Hearing of the proclamation, Chu gave himself up in order to protect other believers. He was executed in 1801 at the age of thirty-two. But his message lived on.

The first Western missionary arrived in 1835. Father Pierre Maubant smuggled himself into the country by crawling through the sewers into the border city of Euiju. Four years later he was beheaded along with two other European priests who had joined him in Korea. By 1865, a dozen priests presided over a community of some 23,000 believers. But the following year another wave of persecution against the Catholic church in Korea cost more than 2,000 Korean Catholics their lives.

After one hundred years of Catholic presence in Korea, there were said to be about 17,500 Catholics living in the country. However, the persecu-

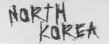

tion against them was so severe that Protestant missionaries entering the country found almost no trace of them.

While the visible church presence had disappeared, the faith was very much alive. The most fearsome persecutor of that era, Prince Regent Tai Won Kun, couldn't even keep Christianity out of his own home. On two occasions a bishop sneaked into the regent's home, first to baptize Kun's wife and then to offer her holy communion. When Kun died in 1898, the Catholic church in Korea had grown to 40,000 members.

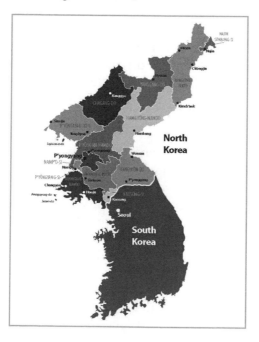

THE FIRST PROTESTANTS

Early Protestant effort in Korea was built on the belief that the Word of God is the greatest witness for Christ. Scripture distribution was the central focus of early mission workers.

In 1832, a German missionary named Carl Gutzlaff sailed along the west coast of Korea for more than a month, witnessing to the people he encountered and passing out religious tracts and Chinese Bibles. He managed to get the Lord's Prayer translated into Korean, but it was not received with any enthusiasm. Koreans who encountered Gutzlaff repeatedly made the motion of their forefinger across their throat. They believed a foreigner in their midst was a great danger to them all. Thirty-three years after Gutzlaff's visit, Robert Thomas became Korea's first Protestant martyr.

The most successful missionaries in the years after Thomas's martyrdom were two Scotsmen who didn't even set foot on Korean soil until many years later. The two men, John Ross and John McIntyre, worked with Koreans in Manchuria, Northern China. They baptized the first Korean Protestants in 1876, and in 1887 they completed the first Korean translation of the New Testament.

One of those first Koreans baptized, Sangyoon Suh, immediately traveled back into Korea, sharing the gospel with his countrymen. Koreans began coming to Christ long before any foreign

Protestant missionaries set up a base on Korean soil.

God used an outbreak of violence and court intrigue to crack open the door for foreign Christian workers. On December 4, 1884, a plot against members of the Korean court exploded into violence. Many of the king's councilors were killed by those seeking to take power. The queen's nephew, Prince Yong-Ik Min, was badly wounded, with seven sword cuts to his head and body. Palace officials called on Dr. Horace N. Allen, a Christian doctor who had come to Korea and been appointed as the physician of the American diplomatic delegation.

Allen worked for three months to save the prince's life, and finally the young man recovered. The king promptly made the Christian doctor the official physician to the Korean royal court. Further, the king decreed that Allen could open a hospital in Seoul in cooperation with "a benevolent society in America." This decree became the first official approval for a Christian organization to work in Korea, a legal foothold for gospel workers, a beachhead from which the gospel advance could be launched throughout the entire country.

Five days before the hospital opened, two missionaries arrived in Korea, landing in the middle of Korea's west coast at Inchon. Rev. Horace Underwood was Presbyterian, while Rev. and Mrs. Henry Appenzeller were Methodists. All were there to bring Korean people to the Light. They made their way to Seoul and began learning the language and quietly planting the seeds of the gospel.

The first Korean baptized on his native soil was Tohsa Noh, who served as Dr. Allen's language teacher. Noh borrowed portions of a Chinese New Testament, even though Allen had advised he would be executed if it was discovered he was reading the book.

Later, Noh went to one of the new missionaries and received more Christian literature. When Noh came back to the missionary and asked to be baptized, the missionary bluntly warned him, "You are going contrary to the law of your country. If you take this step there will be no turning back."

Noh had not been afraid to have a Bible, and he refused to let fear stop him from following his convictions. On July 11, 1886, he was baptized.

The first Protestant church established in Korea was established not by the missionaries but by Koreans. While both Presbyterian and Methodist missionaries were holding services in Seoul, neither wanted to risk offending the government by formally establishing a church congregation. So instead they quietly held services in private homes, working to spread the gospel without raising the ire of Korea's leaders.

With both Protestant groups holding low-key but unofficial services in Seoul, it was a sur-

prise when a Korean arrived in the capital city and asked one of the missionaries to come and baptize believers in a remote coastal village. The Korean was Sang-yoon Suh, one of those baptized by John Ross in Manchuria.

Horace Underwood couldn't immediately travel to the remote village, so Suh returned there. The following spring he arrived back in Seoul and sought out Underwood, this time bringing the new Christian converts with him. The whole mission welcomed them, and convened to examine the new converts. Three were approved as candidates for baptism.

Before the missionaries baptized the three men, they warned them solemnly about the risk they had taken in accepting the gospel and converting to Christianity.

"We are ready to stand by our faith to the death," the men replied. So the service proceeded. With a Methodist missionary guarding the door to make sure the service remained secret, the Presbyterian Underwood baptized the three men from the village of Sorai. A few months later, in the fall of 1887, Underwood went to the village and baptized seven more Korean believers.

The first city churches were also established that fall, as both Methodists and Presbyterians formally founded two congregations in Seoul.

In those early days, it required considerable sacrifice to choose to follow Christ. Korean society was built on the Chinese Confucian tradition (philosophy), which honors family relationships and teaches that ancestors are to be worshiped. For a man to become a Christian was to rob his father and ancestors of their rightful reverence. Male converts were verbally assaulted and sometimes even stoned. Most were disinherited by families who felt they had betrayed their familial duty. Women also faced hardship, as the Confucian ethos demanded loyalty to the husband. Women were beaten and sometimes killed for expressing loyalty to Christ. Yet the church continued to grow.

For the first five years of Protestant work in Korea, the efforts were focused almost exclusively in the capital of Seoul and in the port cities of Inchon on the west coast and Pusan on the southeast corner of the peninsula. After 1890, though, the focus moved inland, and the number of mission groups with an active presence in the country grew exponentially.

The early years of mission work were characterized by a remarkable cooperation between denominations and mission groups. The words of mission worker Dr. W. M. Baird, writing about the establishment of a school in the northern capital of Pyongyang, could be spoken of much of the early work in Korea: "The need was so great that we did not wait for a well-developed scheme or constitution...We simply commenced to cooperate by cooperating. It is better to work

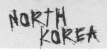
shoulder to shoulder than in disunion and weakness and moral defeat."

The high tide of that spirit of cooperation was a Bible conference held for all missionaries in the summer of 1906. Mission workers made it their aim to establish a unified evangelical church in Korea and left the conference committed to work together to see the goal accomplished.

REVIVAL FIRE BURNS
ACROSS KOREA

Gae-sung, south of Pyongyang, was the first place in Korea noted for widespread spiritual revival. In October 1901, a combined theological symposium was held with Methodists attending from across Korea. From the beginning of the symposium to the end, participants felt in their hearts the "strong descending of the Holy Spirit" calling them to commit themselves anew to the Lord. The Holy Spirit's presence was again clearly felt during a prayer meeting the week before Easter 1902.

In 1903, Wonsan, on the coast directly east of Pyongyang, had a revival. Two female missionaries came together to pray for revival in the city. As their prayer meeting became known, other female Southern Methodist missionaries joined them. The group began to meet regularly for united prayer and Bible study.

Out of that Bible study grew both conviction and confession, and a movement of God's Spirit was evident. Foreign mission workers and Korean believers all sensed it.

During a Sunday morning service, a young man stood to confess his sin. Then another man, Chun-soo Jin, stood and repented of his pride, confessed hidden sexual desires, and repented of his hypocritical behavior. Revival had started. For the next week, a revival meeting was conducted. From all around, Presbyterians, Methodists, and

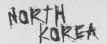

Baptists came to partake of renewal without thought of denominational preferences.

Within a month of that public confession, a special prayer meeting began what was called the Revival of Wonsan. The Holy Spirit manifested His presence with power, and people began to repent of their sin in public. Robert Hardie, who had experienced a renewed infilling and confessed his pride as a missionary and lack of faith, spoke to different gatherings and Bible training classes. The Holy Spirit came upon them, and people repented.

From 1904, Hardie was invited many places across Korea to preach revival messages. During October, he held meetings in Seoul and in Pyongyang. On November 1, he went to Che-mul-po. God moved mightily, and more than a hundred experienced a new infilling of the Holy Spirit. Many missionaries reported they had never seen anything like this before. After 1905, the rapidly spreading revival fires could not be contained in the major cities but spread throughout the nation as people rushed to their hometowns to share the Good News.

In August 1906, resident missionaries in Pyongyang asked Hardie to come and conduct meetings. As the missionaries were preparing through a week-long Bible study and prayer time, they experienced the move of the Holy Spirit. The missionaries all recognized their work was in vain without the leading of the Holy Spirit and only true repentance would bring revival. They began to pray for upcoming winter meetings.

In October, most Korean church leaders came to a mission meeting at Jang-dae-hyun Church in Pyongyang. The main revival speaker, Howard Agnew Johnston, begin to share with them how revival was impacting Wales and India. He spoke of the great movement of God in those countries. As he sat in the audience, Gil Sun-joo experienced the personal touch of the Holy Spirit. He would go on to share revival in other parts of the country.

In the final months of 1906, other outstanding revival movements touched hearts in other cities in different parts of Korea.

The Great Pyongyang Revival of 1907
The Presbyterian and Methodist missionaries in Pyongyang continued to gather to pray for the annual Bible training class to be held in January 1907. The missionaries gathered in prayer every night, pleading for the Holy Spirit to fall upon the class.

Beginning January 2, four Presbyterian groups came together at Jang-dae-hyun Church in Pyongyang for their annual winter Bible training class for men. They held to the normal program: personal meditation time in the early morning, thirty minutes for praising, then three hours of Bible study. After lunch, they went out on the streets to evangelize. At night they gathered for a seekers meeting.

When the evening sessions began four nights later, Elder Gil Sun-joo, who had been so blessed just a few months before by the preaching of Howard Johnston, spoke on repentance. Many people begin to weep, repenting of their sin. Each night God's presence seemed to heat the people up more and more. Six nights later William Blair spoke on 1 Corinthians 12:27 and explained about the need for unity in the Body of Christ. Reconciliation began among the believers.

They were expecting greater things on the following evening, but nothing at all happened. In fact it looked as if God had left. There was a chilly, strange presence in the church. Recognizing a crisis, the missionaries came together in prayer on the morning of January 14. That evening the people prayed in unison. All of a sudden, they begin to cry and pray. It was like Pentecost as described in the Book of Acts. The manifestation of the Holy Spirit was so evident. The work of the Holy Spirit came upon not only Koreans, but also foreign missionaries.

The following evening, the second night of the "Pyongyang Pentecost," Gil Sun-joo stood up to preach. Those who were there noticed a change: His face looked different; he looked holy. He cried out for repentance and sought God for His mercy. People prayed in the same way as on the previous night, but the revival burned upon them even stronger. Church leaders confessed animosity toward each other. People crowded the altar to repent. Many stood up, while others collapsed to the ground. As on the day of Pentecost, the Holy Spirit did the work of conviction and filling.

After that meeting, word spread about what had happened. Many churches desired to see that same revival fire burn in their own congregations. Many who had come to the Bible training class went back to their own churches and witnessed to what they had seen. Some churches began to pray and experienced the descending of the Holy Spirit. When the missionaries returned to their work—be it a school, Bible college, or hospital—the Spirit followed them and fell among them. On February 10, 1907, the Pyongyang Methodist Nam-san-hyun Church received this same revival fire.

After the Pyongyang Revival, Gil Sun-joo went to Seoul to speak at the United Bible Training Class for the Seoul Presbyterian church on February 17. Again, revival came as he proclaimed repentance. He later preached at four more churches in Seoul.

The revival lasted until June 1907, and its witness caused the churches to overflow. In the span of just a few months, the Presbyterian church grew from 14,509 members to 73,847; the Methodists grew from 12,791 to 24,244. The total number of Christians, which had been just a handful in 1885, had grown to around 50,000 in 1905. By 1909, that number had quadrupled.

"MORE LOVE TO THEE"

In 1974, a North Korean newspaper article proclaimed the government had finally killed off the
last remnant of Christian believers in the country.

The article claimed the last remnant was a
group of twenty-nine people who literally lived
under the ground. These brave believers would
sleep underground during the day. At night they
would leave their hiding place to collect tree roots
and other things they could eat.

In 1972, it was announced that Kim Il Sung
would visit a certain village, near the hiding place
of these courageous Christians. Because the "Great
Leader" was afraid of heights and didn't like to fly,
he would need to travel by car; therefore, village
leaders began to work on making a new, top-
quality road for Kim to drive on. During con-
struction, they uncovered the hiding place of the
underground Christians.

When the leaders determined that the people
they had found were followers of "the God of
heaven," four of them were immediately hanged.
The rest were told to lie down on the road, and
the officials ordered a steamroller to run over the
prostrate Christians. To maximize the pain, the
steamroller started by rolling over their feet and
then up toward their heads.

As the Christians awaited their death, one of
them began to sing. Soon the others joined their
voices. The song they sang in Korean was one

familiar to American Christians: "More Love to Thee."

> More love to Thee, O Christ, more love to Thee!
> Hear Thou the prayer I make on bended knee.
> This is my earnest plea: More love, O Christ, to
>   Thee;
> More love to Thee, more love to Thee!
>
> Once earthly joy I craved, sought peace and rest;
> Now Thee alone I seek, give what is best.
> This all my prayer shall be: More love, O Christ
>   to Thee;
> More love to Thee, more love to Thee!
>
> Let sorrow do its work, come grief or pain;
> Sweet are Thy messengers, sweet their refrain,
> When they can sing with me: More love, O
>   Christ, to Thee;
> More love to Thee, more love to Thee!
>
> Then shall my latest breath whisper Thy praise;
> This be the parting cry my heart shall raise;
> This still its prayer shall be: More love, O
>   Christ to Thee;
> More love to Thee, more love to Thee!

These brave Christians had lived underground for almost two decades, choosing to follow Christ instead of a man who said he was a god. One can only imagine the thoughts of Korean officials who watched them die with such courage and dignity, and the welcome these believers must have received in eternity!

DIVISION, COMPROMISE, AND PERSECUTION

The early chapters of Korean church history are marked by great unity among missionaries and churches that bridged denominational and personal backgrounds. However, as time went by, a new generation of missionaries arrived—men and women with different expectations and preparation. The different denominational groups had grown strong enough to support the efforts of individual pastors and missionaries, and the focus shifted from cooperation in evangelism to managing a growing body of believers.

Mission Boards Split

The General Council of Protestant Evangelical Missions of Korea was formed in 1905, with the purpose of the Council "to be a helping body to the Korean Church...the aim of the Council was 'cooperation' in Mission efforts and eventually the organization in Korea of but one native evangelical church." To accomplish this goal of having one church, special meetings were held in 1906, in February and September. Morale among the field missionaries at these meeting was high. Of the 196 missionaries to Korea, 95 percent attended, and the group passed many resolutions toward achieving one evangelical church in Korea.

But many of their home offices had different ideas. The respective denominational headquarters did not understand the missionaries' mind-set and were not supportive of the "one-church concept." Also, the missionaries were bound by their mission boards, so the one-church concept quickly ground to a halt.

Another factor in home-board thinking was the rapid growth of the church after the recent revival. With magnificent reports to share with their national constituencies, funds rolled in. These funds were immediately appointed for special denominational projects. The bigger the projects in Korea, the more closely they were controlled in the missionaries' home countries. Each denomination was busy serving the needs of their growing church bodies in Korea; and the more they served people, the more they felt ownership over their churches. As numbers in each denominational church grew, denominationalism grew as well.

Splits Among the Missionaries

It is tempting to think of missionaries as above reproach, but in reality they have shortcomings and failures like the rest of us. While there were always personal differences among mission workers in Korea, the first evidence of major division among missionaries revolved around status. Missionary stations in Pyongyang and Seoul became divided in 1914 on the issue of college. One-third of the missionaries lived in Seoul, and they wanted to establish a college there since the capital

city was the center for Korean education. However, the remaining two-thirds of the missionaries were located in Pyongyang. The Northern Presbyterians insisted on establishing a college in that city, as did the Southern Presbyterians and some Australian missionaries. The Northern and Southern Methodists wanted the college built in Seoul, while the Canadian Presbyterians took a neutral position. Unable to arrive at a compromise solution on establishing a college, the Methodists broke away from the others in March 1914. The great unity that had led to the growth and revival in the Korean church began to tragically crumble.

Split of Korean Presbyterian and Methodist Churches

When the Federal Council of Protestant Evangelical Missions in Korea was formed in 1912, there was consensus among Presbyterians and Methodists, and the alliance was established. This alliance worked so well that the members wanted to include all evangelical missions under one common umbrella organization. In 1918, the Federal Council of Churches was formed. It was renamed the Korea National Christian Council (KNCC) six years later. The KNCC contained four Presbyterian denominations, two Methodist denominations, the YMCA, the YWCA, the Sunday School Alliance, and the Episcopal denomination. The KNCC did not impose a particular theological stance but generally took a very liberal position.

In addition to liberal-conservative theological differences, as the fiftieth anniversary of Protestant missions to Korea neared, there was a dispute about who was the first missionary to Korea, a foolish argument in light of the Catholics' arrival over a century before. The Methodists held that Reverend R. S. McClay coming from Japan was the first missionary, but the Presbyterians insisted Dr. Allen was first. The stage was set for the Presbyterians to completely disconnect from the Methodists.

As the Methodists celebrated the fiftieth anniversary of their presence in Korea in 1934, the Abingdon Bible Commentary was published. The Presbyterians did not accept this commentary and imposed sanctions against those who read it.

In 1935, the Presbyterians decided to withdraw their membership from the KNCC, further cementing the division between Presbyterians and Methodists. As time went on, mission and church groups worked more and more independently. Further, division developed between Korean Christians and the Western missionaries working in the country.

Compromise: Worship of Other Gods
The most significant division in the Korean church occurred over the issue of bowing to the Japanese Shinto shrines. Shintoism was inter-

twined with Japanese politics and government until after World War II, and included the belief that the Japanese emperor descended from the gods.

Shinto followers erect shrines in many places they consider to be sacred, such as mountains, springs, and rivers. Each shrine is dedicated to a specific *Kami* (god) who has a divine personality and responds to sincere prayers of the faithful. When entering a shrine, one passes through a *Tori*, a special gateway for the gods. It signifies the demarcation between the finite world and the infinite world of the gods. Shrine ceremonies— which include cleansing, offerings, prayers, and dances—are directed to the god.

After Japan annexed Korea in 1910, the government immediately commanded the Japanese church to announce that this annexation was God's will for Japan and that Korea's new status should be accepted by all Christians.

The Japanese government asked the Japanese church to help in colonizing Korea. They were to send Japanese missionaries to plant churches and teach proper Japanese values to Koreans. As part of their enculturation process, the Japanese insisted the conquered Koreans show their respect to Japan's spirit by bowing before their Shinto shrines. The Japanese presented this as a ritual of citizenship devoid of spiritual ramifications. Yet, Shinto worship commemorates the union of the sun goddess and the emperor and presents Japan's emperor as a living god. The Japanese church had long before accepted this compromise position, justifying their submission biblically as a citizen's duty to respect their emperor. Therefore, they denied that it was idol worship. When they arrived in Korea, they began to propagate this unbiblical theology among Korean Christians.

Four years after annexation, Japan mandated that all public school students bow before the Shinto shrine. As the Japanese furthered their imperialistic aspirations in their Manchurian campaign against China, they began imposing Shinto worship on all citizens in occupied lands. They drafted additional military conscripts and forced labor from Korea. Because Western-trained Koreans were the most dangerous to their plans, the Japanese especially targeted Christian schools. After the schools, Korean Christians were next in line.

Police entering one church explained their request simply: "You already worship three Gods —Father, Son, and Holy Ghost. All we ask you to do is add a fourth, the emperor. Why balk at such a little thing?"

Some Christian institutions chose to close rather than compromise. Others feared that their closing would leave Korea without a Christian witness, so they tried to cooperate to prolong their ability to work and witness. Some tried to differentiate between the political nature of ceremonies showing loyalty to Japan and the religious nature of worshiping the emperor. They were tiptoeing on a very fine line.

The Northern Presbyterians very strongly opposed Shinto worship. The Australian Presbyterians determined not to bow to Shinto shrines and began closing their schools in February 1936. The Catholics announced they would accept the imposition as a citizen's ritual and began to bow to Shinto shrines that May. The Southern Presbyterians officially refused to bow on February 2, 1937, preferring instead to close their five hospitals starting that autumn. On June 17, 1937, the Methodists, however, accepted the Shinto ritual as a citizen's act of respect towards their emperor. The Canadian Presbyterians also accepted Shinto worship as a citizen's ritual, at the insistence of Underwood. This allowed them to keep their schools open. The heated debate and the various decisions brought great division among pastors, leaders, and denominations. The Japanese used this division to pressure more churches to submit to Shinto worship.

On September 9, 1938, the historic Presbyterian General Assembly was held at the Seo-moon-eui Church in Pyongyang, with 193 Presbyteries represented by 86 pastors, 85 elders, and 22 missionaries. Each delegate had been interviewed by Japanese police before the meeting and told a measure approving Shinto worship *would* be passed, and voting against it would not be tolerated. Some decided after meeting with the police not to attend the assembly, but police would not allow them to abstain from the vote and forcibly escorted them to the church. Under such pressure, the assembly voted to approve the bowing to Shinto shrines without allowing debate or dissent.

Shim Ik-hyun of the Pyongyang Fellowship of Pastors made a motion that all those at the meeting should go to the Pyongyang Shinto Shrine. At noon, the Vice Chair of the organization led 23 Presbytery heads down to the shrine and then in a worship ceremony.

This historic compromise gave the Japanese a club with which to beat the resistance out of the Korean church. Many Korean Christians believe it also set in motion the struggles, persecution and oppression that continue today in North Korea. Today, on the site where the Presbyterian General Assembly was held, there stands a giant statue of Kim Il Sung, as if commemorating a pact with the devil.

Split Among Korean Christians

Many Korean Christians individually opposed bowing to the Shinto shrines, even though their church leaders had compromised. Those who expressed their opposition were jailed, and many died in prison. Others chose not to suffer and accepted Shinto worship as a citizen's ritual. This was especially common among those of liberal theology. Many pastors and leaders with high visibility were busy pleasing the Japanese.

The compromised church was no longer a community of faith but a tool of the Japanese propaganda machine to promote and support Japanese imperialism. Church artifacts and equipment were "given" to the Japanese so they could make them into weapons. Collections were taken up for purchasing warplanes. Some churches were pressured to sell their land and buildings and "donate" the proceeds to the war fund. Forty church buildings, including the Nam-san-hyun Church of Pyongyang, were sold along with land to meet the required war fund contribution amount. The Korean church was divided, with part of it willingly conceding its spiritual authority to the gods of Japan.

With the compromise of so many Christians, the persecution grew more intense against those who still refused to bow to the shrines. In the years leading up to World War II, more than two hundred churches were closed, two thousand believers put in prison, and fifty pastors tortured almost to the point of death for refusing to bow.

Many Christians simply went underground, escaping to mountain villages or practicing their Christian faith only in private.

Missionaries Expelled

Though some missionaries accepted the imposition of Japanese Shinto worship and bowed to the shrines, many were adamantly opposed. They were again divided among themselves. As the world rushed headlong into war, the United States government ordered all Americans, including missionaries, to leave Korea. The Japanese also put pressure on the missionaries to leave, viewing them as "foreign spies." On November 11, 1940, the first batch of 160 missionaries and 49 children left. Forty more were deported in April 1941. H. H. Underwood, son of one of the original missionaries, was the last missionary to leave Korea, staying until June 1, 1942, six months after the Japanese attack on Pearl Harbor and the formal declaration of war.

With the foreign missionaries gone, the leadership of the church was left fully in the hands of Koreans. The seduction of these leaders, as well as the persecution of those who refused to be seduced, continued.

In July 1943, church leaders from across the country attended the first assembly of leaders of the "Korean Christian Church of Japanese Christianity." At the opening session, the church leaders were led by a Shinto priest on a procession to the Han River for a Shinto ceremony of purification, which was yet another show of compromise.

In spite of such ceremonies and meetings, the Japanese occupiers never trusted Korean Christians. The Japanese governor over the country told one observer: "There is one army of over 400,000 who are not afraid of death. They are the Christians." Because of Japanese distrust, many pastors were arrested, including some who had cooperated with the Japanese and bowed to the Shinto shrines.

It was later learned that many of the church leaders were scheduled for execution on August 18, 1945. Their lives were saved by the dropping of the atomic bombs on Nagasaki and Hiroshima and the subsequent ending of the war. When Emperor Hirohito announced the Japanese surrender ending World War II on August 15, the church leaders were allowed to go free—three days before their executions were scheduled to occur.

TESTIMONY

"Roli"

VOM workers met with "Roli," a Chinese Christian woman who is working inside North Korea, in 2005. Here is her story:

I became a Christian in 1990. My husband and I first went to the official church, but we wanted to learn freely. So in 1993, we started a home church in the second floor of our home with eight of our Christian friends.

My husband passed away in 1996. He was a believer but not very strong in his faith. When he died, I began to blame God. I was really depressed and lonely.

The more I prayed about my situation, the more I felt God calling me to North Korea. So in the spring of 1997, I planned my first trip. My children were very upset. They said it was too dangerous, but I had to see if this was indeed God's calling.

The moment I stepped foot in North Korea, my depression went away. I felt an inner peace I hadn't felt in many years. I knew God had called me here, but then I was heartbroken by what I saw.

I walked down the road in this one village where dead bodies were on the side of the road. I saw a hungry boy eating one of the bodies. But then a policeman also saw him, and pulling out his revolver, he shot the boy in the head. It was the first but not the last person I saw shot for cannibalism in North Korea.

When I returned to China after my first trip, I left something in North Korea—my heart. I knew this was to be my ministry, so I made frequent trips and began a network of people to evangelize. You can bring small gifts, some food, a toy, or even pencils and paper. The North Koreans warm up to you, and I would look for opportunities to share the gospel.

Once they believed in Jesus I would come back for training and try to bring them a Bible. Since my first trip in 1997, I have made contact with forty house churches and helped start another sixty.

But now the work is very difficult. The larger it gets, the more dangerous it is. Our first arrest happened in 1999. Four believers were caught worshiping together. They were arrested and sentenced to seven years. A young man who was trained extensively and active in the Bible delivery was recently arrested. He has disappeared. I am really worried about him as well.

Another family was arrested—the whole family, including the children. They are all in prison except for the father. He was executed.

Some former prisoners have died from their imprisonment. The guards let prisoners go when they are near death. They usually die within a few weeks or months of their release.

Just this year a family was arrested. The parents were taken to one prison and the children to another. Officials burned their house down. I helped two children (a son and daughter) of one family to get into China for more training. But they were caught returning to North Korea. They were charged with "treason" and becoming "Christians," and have been publicly executed. This is the saddest for me. I was very close to this family.

I am sorry it is difficult for me to share more. So many have been arrested, so many killed.

EDITOR'S NOTE: *At the time of this printing, Roli continues her work inside North Korea. Please pray for her work, as it is extremely dangerous. She is in her mid seventies. Before concluding the interview, Roli was asked if she had any idea of the extent of the ministry going on inside North Korea. She could not even guess but said, "I know there are many people doing what I do. I see them coming across the border. No one ever speaks a word, but you just know who they are. They have wings."*

SHORT-LIVED FREEDOM

Korean Christians deliriously greeted the "free-dom" brought to them by the liberation of Korea at the end of World War II. Christians poured into the streets, joyously singing hymns that had been banned by the Japanese. Prisoners held in Pyongyang, including an estimated 20,000 Christians, were released only days before many of them were scheduled to be executed. Instead of going home, the Christians went to San-jung-hyun Church for a service of thanksgiving. With great rejoicing, the churches reopened on August 22. A provisional Presbytery meeting was called the following month, and three days of fasting and prayer for repentance of the Korean nation was scheduled.

Little did these believers know that the persecution they'd endured under the Japanese was just a prelude for the deadly war against the church that was about to be waged.

At the end of World War II, the Korean peninsula was divided at the 38th parallel. The Soviets occupied the northern half, with the U.S. Army occupying the southern half. At the time of occupation, the stated plan was to quickly establish a unified Korean nation and withdraw the occupying forces.

Northern Presbyterians formed a temporary Northern General Assembly, pending reunion with churches in the South, from whom they had been cut off by the division of the country. An evangelistic campaign was launched. The Presbyterian seminary in Pyongyang, which had closed in protest over the Shinto worship ceremonies, was reopened. Dr. W. N. Blair, the only missionary allowed briefly into Russian-occupied North Korea, found 164 students in attendance at the seminary in 1947.

Those pastors who had been jailed for refusing to bow to Shinto shrines met together with a goal to purify the church and restore those pastors who had compromised their faith. The pastors agreed to a five-point plan that called for pastors who had bowed to Shinto shrines to take time off from preaching ministry—at least two months—for reflection and repentance. Churches were instructed to enact this immediately. Further, they agreed to immediately reopen the seminary for the training of additional pastors.

On November 14, 1945, two hundred ministers gathered for the Presbytery meeting. Their time served as a revival. They were praying and praising the Lord with great thanksgiving for their liberation from the Japanese. In the midst of the revival, the five-point plan was brought before the group to be adopted and implemented. When the plan was brought up for discussion, the pastor who had chaired the movement to bow to Shintoism, Pastor Hong Tack-ki, immediately opposed these statements, saying:

The pains and sufferings of the persons who were in jail and the persons who bent a little to keep the church in existence are the same. Those who were pressured daily by the Japanese and eventually coerced should be evaluated higher than those who abandoned the flock and fled overseas.

It is each person's responsibility, between God and that person, and it should be handled directly by themselves, whether they bowed to Shintoism and need to repent and accept punishment or not.

Emboldened by the pastor's defense, those present who had compromised by bowing to idols refused to repent. The meeting ended without any church or even a single Presbytery resolving to implement the five-point rule for church repentance and revival. Instead, those accused were defensive; the accusers were hurt and angry. This spirit of division created distance and disputes between pastors and among the congregations that they led.

For the sake of unity among all the members of the Presbytery, those present made a compromise at the human level. Instead of moving ahead in helping the compromised pastors find reconciliation with the rest, they shifted directions and decided to unite behind an anti-communist stance. Even though national and public repentance was needed and encouraged, spiritual reconciliation was neglected.

The Methodists had their first post-war annual meeting in 1945. At that meeting the issue was not even raised about the church bowing to the Japanese shrines. By June 1945, there were 2,346 Shinto shrines in Korea. Because almost all Methodist pastors had, in fact, bowed before Shinto and actively cooperated with the Japanese government to retain their posts and mission property, there was no mention of the need to repent.

A HYMN FOR NORTH KOREA

The following is a translation of the words sung by a young North Korean Christian who had escaped into China. His heart's desire was to take the message of the gospel back to his homeland.

Once upon a time in the East, there was the bright city of Jerusalem.

How come the city has been ruined? The Lord is saddened by it.

Oh Lord! Send us to them, to our beloved brothers in the North,

Oh Lord! Send us to them, to our beloved brothers in the North,

Help us pray more than ever before.

Oh Lord! Give us the voice of the gospel for our beloved brothers the Lord so loved before.

Where are all these gone? The Lord is looking upon them.

Oh Lord! Send us to them, to our beloved Korean brothers.

Oh Lord! Send us to them, to our beloved Korean brothers.

Wherever they are, let them bloom as flowers.

Oh Lord! Give us the voice of the gospel!

One young sheep is more precious than sky and land.

The Lord will restore so many sheep that went
astray.

Oh Lord! Send us there for our own people in
the Fatherland.

Oh Lord! Send us there for our own people in
the world.

Let them be a pillar of fire to shine to the
entire world.

Oh Lord! Give us the voice of the gospel!

*North Koreans gather for Bible study at a
secret safe house in China sponsored by VOM.*

THE COMMUNIST TAKEOVER

Even before Liberation Day and the end of Japanese occupation, Russian troops had crossed into Korea. Joseph Stalin's master plan was that the entire world would become communist.

On September 19, 1945, Kim Il Sung and a band of Korean communists arrived at Wonsan aboard a Russian vessel called the *Pugachof*, which had sailed from the Russian city of Vladivostok. The vessel was welcomed to port by two Russian officers.

The man calling himself Kim Il Sung was in fact a thirty-three-year-old Korean named Kim Sung Joo. He had been actively organizing the Communist Party since earlier that year. He was the man the Russians had chosen to lead their half of Korea, and hopefully to unite the peninsula under the communist doctrines.

Kim Sung Joo was the son of two Christian parents and had been educated in what is now China's Jilin province. After his schooling, he worked twenty years for the Chinese and Soviet Communists Parties. His oldest son, Kim Jong Il, was born in Soviet territory where his father was working for the Russians. Korean propaganda today claims that Kim Jong Il's birth was actually in Korea, and that the day was marked by a double rainbow over Mt. Paektu.

The true Kim Il Sung was a grand old general, a war hero who had bravely fought against the

Japanese. He had disappeared from public life in 1942.

When it was announced that "Kim Il Sung" would return to Pyongyang on October 14, 1945, 60,000 people turned out to welcome the aged warrior. Instead they found a much younger man, one who pretended to be the great general. The Chinese- and Russian-educated imposter had such poor Korean language skills that he had to be coached before making speeches to Korean audiences. Yet his backing from the Soviet troops made it impossible for the people to call his bluff.

Four months later, Kim Il Sung was elected chairman of the North Korean Provisional People's Committee. This seventeen-member committee included twelve Communist Party members. Among their platforms was a plank giving the Committee the right to operate as a government in North Korea. This was the real beginning of communist control of the people of the North.

The following month, the communists passed a "land reform act," which called for anyone with more than five hectares (500 acres) of land to turn the excess over to the government. Christians, however, were labeled as "anti-revolutionary," "anti-people," and "anti-nationalist," and so the government confiscated all property belonging to religious organizations.

Some people think Kim was opposed to Christians from the start of his regime, but in fact, he initially tried to work with the Christians to

increase his power base. Trained by Russian communists, he knew of their success in using the Orthodox Church to influence people in Russia.

Several events changed Kim's mind and turned him violently against the Christians. The first was the formation of two Christian political parties, which pressed for more freedom and worked against communism's rise to power.

The second event involved a celebration of the March 1st Independence Movement in 1946. The communists organized a rally in Pyongyang, where they hoped a massive turnout would solidify and strengthen the Communist Party. However, churches decided to conduct their own celebrations of the day apart from the communist rally. Police discovered their plan and arrested sixty pastors in an effort to stop the Christian service. When five thousand Christians showed up for the rally, the main speaker was arrested. The Christians moved into the streets shouting for more freedom and demanding the Russian troops leave Korea.

The final blow to any chance Kim saw of working through churches came that same day. While Kim was speaking at the communist rally in front of the Pyongyang Railroad Station, someone threw a hand grenade onto the platform. It is unknown who actually threw the grenade, but it was easy for Kim to blame dissenting Christians after the disturbance at the Christian rally earlier that day.

Less than two weeks later, in two separate incidents, young Christians threw bombs at the home of Pastor Kang Yang-uk. Pastor Kang, a graduate of Pyongyang Seminary, had served as a Presbyterian pastor and an evangelist prior to the communist takeover. Kang had enjoyed good relationships with other pastors and Christian leaders. He had also taught at Chang-duk School, where one of his students had been Kim Il Sung. In fact, Kang was the only man in the country whom Kim addressed as "teacher," a term of great honor in Asian culture.

Some Christians, including the two who threw bombs at Kang's house, thought that because of his relationship with Kim Il Sung, he could have prevented the crackdown against the church on March 1. Their outburst resulted in the death of two of Kang's children and effectively closed the ears of the only Christian to whom Kim Il Sung would listen. Instead of being an advocate on behalf of the churches, Kang became embittered. From the point of the bombings, Kang attacked fellow pastors unless they joined the communist movement.

That fall Kim called for a general election to form the communist government. He set the date of the election as November 3, 1946, a Sunday. The Five Province United Presbytery opposed holding an election on a Sunday and formally petitioned Kim to change the date of the vote. The request was denied, and Pastor Kang issued a statement in support of the Sunday election. On the day of the vote, many churches encouraged their parishioners to remain in church until the polls had closed. Church leaders saw this as an act of protest. Communist leaders saw it as insurrection, solidifying their view that Christians were untrustworthy and uncooperative. Many Christians who chose not to vote in the election were arrested and interrogated by police.

The communists sought control of the church in three stages. First, they broke political organizations away from the church, closing down groups that were led by known Christians or that espoused Christian principles. These groups, the communists knew, would push for more freedom for Korea's people and would buck against communist rule. Two political movements led by Christians, the Social Democratic Party and the Christian Liberal Party, were both quashed by the communists.

Secondly, the communist regime tried to enslave the church and force church leaders to support it. The regime formed the "Christian League" and made membership mandatory for church officials. The Methodist and Presbyterian seminaries were forcibly combined into one "Christian Seminary." Under government pressure to limit the number of students, seminary enrollment declined from 1,200 to 120.

Under the direction of Pastor Kang, the Korean Christian Federation was born on November 28, 1946. It was formed as a nondenominational entity that could encompass both Protestant and Catholic church leaders. One-third of North Korean pastors joined the Federation. Those who refused were soon deleted from membership in local Presbyteries and began to suffer persecution at the hands of communist leaders.

Thirty months after Kim Il Sung was elected leader of the Provisional People's Committee, he solidified his power and was elected the first Prime Minister. The official birthday of the Democratic People's Republic of Korea was September 9, 1948.

By 1950, the communists had lost confidence in their ability to control the church. Seeing that some Christians would rather die than be controlled by a godless government, they moved into the final stage of their offensive: extermination.

A propaganda painting shows Kim Il Sung caring for soldiers by helping one tie his boot.

조선화 《남진의 길에서 병사들의 행군을 돌보아주시는 최고사령관 김일성원수님》 직 성신, 오 광 호
朝鮮画 《嗷高司令官金日成同志体貼向南行军的战士》 金哲振、呉光浩

Church buildings were confiscated. Pastors were put in prison.

At that time Kim turned his attention to greater conquests. The Korean War broke out on June 25, 1950, when thousands of North Korean troops broke across the 38th parallel, which had been the dividing line between North and South Korea. U.S. troops had withdrawn from South Korea after an independent government was established there. Kim Il Sung did not think the U.S. would send troops again into the land and thought a quick strike would unify all of Korea under his leadership.

In mid June, North Korea assembled some 90,000 men supported by 150 Soviet tanks near the 38th Parallel. On June 25, the North Koreans launched a coordinated attack that spanned from coast to coast. The South Korean army numbered 95,000 on that day. By the end of the month, they could account for only 22,000 men.

United Nations (U.N.) forces, including thousands of U.S. troops brought in from Japan, joined the conflict under the leadership of General Douglas MacArthur. They pushed the North Korean troops all the way back to the Chinese border. Thousands of Chinese troops crossed into Korea to bolster Kim's communist forces, and pushed the U.N. troops back, retaking Pyongyang in December and Seoul the following month. The U.N. forces recaptured Seoul in March, and by July the front had stabilized along what is today the border between North and South Korea. The two sides signed a cease-fire agreement in July 1953 but have never signed a formal peace agreement and today remain technically at war.

U.S. history books call this disagreement the "Korean Conflict" or "Korean Police Action," since a formal declaration of war was never passed by Congress. South Koreans call it the "June 25th Incident" or the "Korean War." In North Korea, it is known as the "Fatherland Liberation War."

During the war, as communist troops retreated, they often massacred Christians to keep them from being liberated by oncoming South Korean, U.N., and American forces. It was one more way to wipe the gospel presence from Korean soil.

As the South Korean and American troops

pushed the communist army back and liberated Pyongyang and other cities, celebration worship services were held by Christians in many places. Sometimes American military chaplains or officers were asked to speak in churches as the Korean citizens welcomed their liberators.

This propaganda poster says "If we start an aggressive war, we will strike America (wretch) first!"

74

This propaganda poster says "Unmerciful punishment to the Empire of America!"

In the minds of the communists, though, this solidified their view of Christians as pro-American, anti-communist, and anti-revolutionary. When communists recaptured Pyongyang, many Koreans who attended these services paid a deadly price.

Having seen the oppression of Kim's communist regime, many Christians fled as American forces retreated, knowing there would be no freedom in a communist North Korea. In the months after the Chinese troops crossed the Yalu River to assist their communist brethren on the battlefield, more than 4 million North Koreans fled to the South. Many arrived with nothing more than the clothes on their backs. Thousands of North Korean troops captured during the battles refused to return to the North when the war ended, choosing instead the freedom of the South.

Church losses during the Korean War were devastating. One researcher reports that 1,373 churches were completely destroyed with more than 650 others partially damaged. Noticing that American bombers didn't target churches and religious buildings, communists used the buildings to store military goods and weapons. They placed anti-aircraft guns outside of churches, and consequently several churches were bombed, sometimes with people inside. North Korean propaganda today teaches that the U.S. purposefully bombed the churches to kill innocent people.

In addition to church buildings, the communists also specifically targeted church leaders. Kim Yoon-chan, a former pastor from Pyongyang, reported how pastors were dealt with: "At the beginning of the Korean War, the North Korean regime killed all the pastors who were members of the Korean Christian Federation in one night. Since they had no use for these pastors, they put them in a warehouse and set it on fire to kill them cruelly. Fifty-three other pastors were also killed near the Dae-dong River."

Estimates vary greatly about the number of Christians remaining after the war. One researcher says there were 300,000 Christians in North Korea at the end of World War II. Persecution reduced that number to 200,000 in the next five years, and to 100,000 after the Korean War ended. Of those who remained, as many as 50 percent denied their faith because of the intense persecution and turned instead to communism. North Korean statistics say there were only 12,000 Christians in North Korea at the end of the Korean War. More accurate estimates are that 50,000 existed, but 80 percent of them worshiped underground to avoid communist persecution.

QUOTABLE:

"In the years I was in prison, I saw many believers die. Yet they never, never denied the God who is in heaven. All they had to do was say they don't believe in religion and they would have been released.
I didn't understand what made them not fear death. Their unbelievable faith brought a big question into my heart: What did they see, and what am I missing?"

—SOON OK LEE, *Eyes of the Tailless Animals*
(After her release from prison, Lee escaped from North Korea and later met a Christian man who gave her a Bible. Today she too is one of the "heaven people," the derogatory name given to Christians by the North Korean government.)

THE UNDERGROUND CHURCH

After the Korean War, the communist government set about to "purify" the country and eliminate all those who might oppose the regime. During this time the visible church was completely eradicated from North Korean society. Church buildings were converted to other purposes or simply demolished into piles of rubble. Recent research indicates there were 3,025 churches when the communists took over the country. By 1955, that number was zero.

From 1953 to 1972, no Christian activities were allowed by the North Korean regime. Even the Korean Christian Federation formed by Pastor Kang, the man Kim Il Sung called "teacher," was not allowed to function.

During these years anyone found to be a Christian faced one of two punishments: either execution or a harsh sentence such as long years of "re-education" in a labor camp or coal mine. Christians faced complete social rejection, as no one wanted to risk the regime's wrath by interacting with a Christian. Most of the labor camps where Christians were held—and died—during this period are still functioning today.

An ally of Kim Il Sung wrote that by 1958 all Christians had been captured, and that the only way to change the behavior of Christians was to kill them. Praise God for the faithfulness of North

Korean believers who faced death rather than renounce their faith in Christ!

In 1966, the government divided the citizenry into 51 social classifications. Christians were assigned classification #37—though the government claimed all Christians had been arrested by 1958.

In 1967, Kim Il Sung ordered all books in the country to be burned or donated to the libraries. Library books couldn't be checked out, only accessed inside the library building after providing identification to the librarian. Only the writings of Kim Il Sung were widely available in the country. Some Christians burned their Bibles out of fear of the regime; others hid them. In the years following this "Little Cultural Revolution," many were executed simply for being in possession of a Bible. Today if North Koreans are found with a Bible, they—along with their parents and children—are sentenced to fifteen years in the labor camps. This is the regime's attempt to wipe out three generations of "disloyal" families.

One VOM contact met a young woman during a visit to North Korea. With tears the woman shared her story. One day when she was nine years old, her class was given a special assignment by their teacher. The students were instructed to go home and look for a black, nicely bound book. The teacher didn't say what the book was, only that their parents would probably have it hidden somewhere in the house.

The teacher instructed them not to tell their parents of their assignment but simply to look for the black-bound book. And if they found one, they were to bring it to school the next day.

This young girl looked carefully in her house, and did in fact find a nice leather-bound book like the teacher had described. She carefully hid it in her bag, not telling her parents, and took it to school the following day. She was very proud to stand up in front of the class and tell the teacher she had completed the extra assignment by bringing the book with her.

The book she'd found was a Bible.

When that nine-year-old girl arrived home that day, her parents were gone. In fact, she told our contact she had not seen or heard from them since that day. She assumed they were killed because of the Bible she had found. Many years later she also became a follower of Jesus.

During the darkest days of the "Little Cultural Revolution," the North Korean government claimed to have completely destroyed the church. But Christians carried on discretely in worship and ministry. Some moved to very remote areas to try to avoid detection; others lived underground. It is impossible to get an accurate count of how many Christians there were during this period or how many died for their faith in Christ. There are stories, though, about the persecution faced by Christ's followers.

One pastor was leading more than two thousand believers, divided into more than five hundred small groups. For security he could meet with only three to five believers at a time. The pastor was caught when police raided a home where he was holding a meeting. He was executed publicly with ten other Christian leaders in 1958. The believers he shepherded were dispersed around North Korea. Many were sent to the remote, mountainous regions in the far northern area of the country.

One man was thought to be a good communist, though some police were suspicious of him. They told him he had to move to a different town but gave him a few minutes to pack, enough time for him to dig his Bible and a hymnbook out of a hole in the ground and secretly stow them into his luggage. But before he was allowed to leave, his luggage was searched. Police tortured the pastor into giving up the names of other believers, then continued the cycle of torture until most Christians in the area had been found and executed.

Despite the regime's efforts to wipe out Christianity, the gospel message lived on. Korean Christians returned from living in Japan and China, bringing the gospel message with them. Others simply remained true in spite of the danger and persecution. One woman said she prayed in a secret place in her attic where she would not be spotted, every day *for twenty-seven years*. The woman knelt in silent prayer all those years, unable to cry out audibly to God for fear her faith would be discovered. Instead, she prayed silently, her body twisting back and forth, until she had literally worn grooves in the wooden floor with her knees.

Recently, one mission group did a study of archived material, and found 441 reports of persecution from 1945 until 2005. This did not include every case but only those the ministry had documented in some way. The information concerned 4,562 North Koreans and what happened to those who were exposed as Christians. Nearly 20 percent of the cases involved either a small group of believers or a network of such groups, proving the regime's claims to have wiped out the church are not true. Most of the cases—more than 93 percent—involved not pastors or church leaders but lay members.

Of those discovered to be Christians, 89 percent either were executed or simply disappeared. Only one-half of 1 percent—five out of every thousand—were allowed to return to their homes. Almost six hundred of those martyred for their faith were killed after 1972, the time when North Korea's government leaders thought they had killed or "re-educated" every Christian in the country.

The data in this study is not comprehensive. It was simply what could be gathered from media reports and interviews with North Korean defectors. However, it does show the continued presence of Christian believers in North Korea as well as their continued persecution and suffering. Kim Il Sung and his regime either executed or abducted 89 percent of those discovered to be Christian, and yet they could not wipe out the gospel message from their nation. God's faithfulness to His children remains. The underground church is alive and well, and the Holy Spirit continues to minister and grow Christ's Body in the Hermit Kingdom.

The Official Church
While the North Koreans tried to wipe out the church from their soil, they recognized that in South Korea the church was growing and becoming an important part of South Korean society. When the two countries began talks in 1972, Kim Il Sung knew many South Koreans were Christians and could identify with Christians in North Korea. Because of this, he allowed some religious activities to begin again, purely as a negotiating tool with South Korea.

After being closed for twenty-two years, a seminary was opened in Pyongyang. Ten students were allowed to study for three years. The seminary was a part of Pastor Kang's effort to reactivate the Korean Christian Federation (KCF) in order to receive aid from foreign nations. The KCF was officially reactivated in August 1973, and applied for membership in the World Council of Churches a year later. The Council denied membership, saying there was no evidence of the existence of Christians in North Korea.

To gain membership in the WCC, the government trained people to act as Christian believers and even constructed a church building for foreign visitors to see.

These moves did not come about because Kim Il Sung or his government had changed their opinion of Christianity. They were simply cosmetic changes to attract foreign aid and help North Korea gain a negotiating advantage.

In one case a carpenter was brought in to construct a church building in Pyongyang. When the building was finished, the carpenter was assigned to be the pastor there.

At a 1986 meeting in Switzerland, the KCF reported one seminary, 18 pastors, 500 house churches, and 10,000 believers, including Catholics. In 2000, the official numbers reported were 30 ordained pastors and 300 church staff serving a total of 12,000 believers.

It is difficult to know if any of those worshiping in the official church are truly born again and have a personal relationship with Jesus. One aid group visiting Pyongyang was taken to two different Protestant churches for services during their visit. Members of the group said the same "church choir" was singing in both services!

TESTIMONY

Miss Kul

Miss Kul was interviewed by VOM workers along the North Korean border with China. This is part of her story.

I was caught trying to escape and sentenced to one month and ten days in jail, along with fifteen other women. We went to a special prison camp that was just for those caught trying to escape. It is a miracle I am alive. I did not think I would survive the prison. They treated us worse than animals.

We had no water. We began work at 5:00 a.m. and worked until 4:30 p.m. Then we immediately went into "training" and more work until 11:00 p.m. and then more training. We had no water during this time. And if they got mad at us, they took away the little food we were supposed to receive. (We were fed bare corn cobs.)

They liked to beat us with rubber whips, which were about 3 feet long and flat on one side. Prisons who were too weak to meet their quota were whipped more, making it more difficult for them to work and meet their quotas, so the cycle repeated. We felt very bad for them.

After work and training, we were put in these small cells—fifty of us in one room. We had to sleep in shifts because there wasn't enough room for all of us to lie down at the same time.

After our one month and ten days was up, the ladies arrested with me were released together —all except one woman. We do not know what happened to her. She disappeared.

She was wearing a cross.

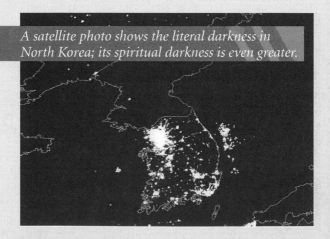

A satellite photo shows the literal darkness in North Korea; its spiritual darkness is even greater.

JUCHE

It is impossible to discuss the condition of the church and the persecution of Christians in North Korea without also discussing Juche, the philosophy that underlies North Korea's government and way of life.

The propagandists of North Korea would have the world believe Juche is nothing more than a philosophical idea. The word itself is best translated "self-reliance." But it is far more than a philosophy, more than Kim Il Sung's version of Marxist-Leninist thought. It is an oppressive spiritual system—a *religion*—that exists to keep the people of North Korea in bondage under government control. The deification of the "Great Leader" Kim Il Sung, who died in 1994, and his son, Kim Jong Il, the "Dear Leader," is a central part of their strategy to maintain power.

The philosophy is taught to all citizens from the nursery to the nursing home. Pre-school children are taught to sing what can only be described as "worship choruses" to Kim Il Sung and Kim Jong Il. Those who express beliefs contrary to Juche, including the belief in "the God of heaven," are taken for re-education or are executed.

Most of the world's people know nothing about Juche. Many have never even heard the term. Yet with more than 20 million practitioners, it ranks ahead of Judaism on a list of world religions.

Kim Jong Il described Juche this way: "Living in the Korean way means thinking with our own heads, acting and solving everything with our own strength according to the interests of our country's revolution and people, as demanded by the Juche idea."

But what is the Juche idea? According to researcher Thomas Belke, "Juche's central teachings exist solely to promote and sustain the totalitarian regime of Kim Jong Il." Belke goes on to list the five primary goals of the Juche ideology:

1. The justification of Kim Jong Il as dictator-god

2. Hereditary power succession

3. Xenophobic isolationism

4. National reunification (Kim Jong Il's rule over all of Korea)

5. Export of the Juche system on a worldwide basis

North Korea's constitution promises that the government will make Juche ideology the guiding principle for every action it takes and every decision it makes. The following table, from Belke's book *Juche: A Christian Study of North Korea's State Religion*, examines some of the teachings of this philosophy/religion.

North Koreans must wear a pin with the face of Kim Il Sung.

Some Core Teachings of the Juche Religion

Juche Doctrine	Corresponding Teaching*
Leader worship	Kim Il Sung and Kim Jong Il are divine, immortal, and worthy of all prayer, worship, honor, power, and glory.
Totalitarian subordination of the individual to the nation	The individual must guide all his or her actions according to the Juche ideal as revealed by the immortal Comrade Kim Jong Il. Juche is "the socialist cause of Korean style, is the cause of national independence which places the destinies of the country and nation ahead of other things and subordinates everything to it."
Man as the beginning and end of all things	"The revolutionary cause of Juche started by President Kim Il Sung and being carried forward to completion by Secretary Kim Jong Il is the revolutionary cause of genuine national independence started and advanced by the Korean people with their own faith and will."
Self-validation	"The revolutionary cause of Juche has become the cause of genuine national independence because it has been led by President Kim Il Sung and Secretary Kim Jong Il."
Korea ethnocentrism	"This is the sacred country. As a result of Juche, the powerful so-

* *From the Korean Central News Agency, Democratic Peoples Republic of Korea.*

Some Core Teachings *(continued)*

Juche Doctrine	Corresponding Teaching
	cialist country, strong in the Juche character and national character and independent in politics, self-supporting in the economy and self-reliant in national defense, has been built in this land."
	"Because of our Party, the position of our country has been raised beyond comparison, and the dignity and honor of the nation shine all over the world."
	"The Korean people are blessed most in the world with the peerless great man comrade Kim Jong Il whom they have held in high esteem as the leader of the WPK [Worker's Party of Korea]."
North Korea is "paradise on earth"	North Korea, despite her ongoing "struggle," is paradise on earth. Other nations, such as "the South," which do not have the benefit of Juche, are poor, miserable places to live.
Juche is uniquely Korean	"All the lines and policies of the Korean revolution which have been shaped and pursued historically have never been based on the established theories or experience of others."
Reunification	Reunification of the divided Korean peninsula along Juche guidelines

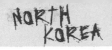
Some Core Teachings *(continued)*

Juche Doctrine	Corresponding Teaching
	is not only a political agenda, but a sacrosanct principle of Juche religion. "Juche is the cause of national reunification…the revolutionary cause of genuine national independence."
Extreme national self-reliance	"It is the Korean people's way of making revolution and their basic stand to push ahead with the revolution and construction with their own viewpoint, will and decision and to hold fast to independence in external relations."
Interdependence brings disaster	Any calamity can be attributed to improper reliance on other nations. "The WPK and the Korean people have held high the banner of self-reliance, mindful that dependence on outside forces leads to the collapse of the country and self-reliance guarantees the prosperity of the country and nation."
The cause of Juche will ultimately be victorious	"The revolutionary cause of Juche is the cause of self-reliance which emerges victorious ever by the efforts of the Korean people… Juche is the nation-loving struggle to establish the sovereignty of the nation throughout the country and guarantee the welfare of posterity for all ages."

Juche's domination of the people of North Korea is total. Information is completely controlled, so most citizens believe that, even in their dire poverty, they are better off than the rest of the world. They are told—and many believe—their country is truly a paradise on earth.

When Belke asked the editor of the Korean Central News Agency for a concise, "non-psychobabble" definition of Juche, the result was an exact quote from Kim Jong Il's book, *On the Juche Idea of Our Party:*

> The Juche idea is a new philosophical thought which centers on man. The Juche idea is based on the philosophical principle that man is the master of everything and decides everything. The Juche idea raised the fundamental question of philosophy by regarding man as the main factor, and elucidated the philosophical principle that man is the master of everything and decides everything. That man is the master of everything means that he is the master of the world and his own destiny; that man decides means that he plays the decisive role in transforming the world and in shaping his destiny. The philosophical principle of the Juche idea is the principle of man-centered philosophy which explains man's position and role in the world.

Based on this, it is easy to see how the followers of Juche's humanism would view those who follow the omniscient, omnipresent, all-powerful Creator God: with animosity and even hatred.

Through the Juche religious system, Belke writes, Kim Il Sung was proclaimed the immortal God and eternal Father, with miraculous powers. One example is a story published in 1963 about the crew of the fishing boat *Minchungho*. Threatened by a storm, the crew gathered in the captain's cabin and began to chant excerpts from Kim Il Sung's biography, especially about his valiant struggle against the Japanese. The storm, according to the story, miraculously subsided. There are also numerous stories of the sun breaking through the clouds upon Kim's arrival at a given location or of flowers bursting into bloom around him.

The Party openly describes Kim Il Sung as a god. Kim is, according to one writer, "superior to Christ in love, superior to Buddha in benevolence, superior to Confucius in virtue and superior to Mohammed in justice." The official eulogy after his death said, "The sun of the nation ... not only protected the political life of the people but also saved their physical life, his love cured the sick and gave them a new life, like the spring rain falling on the sacred territory of Korea."

By his eightieth birthday, there were 70 bronze statues of him in North Korea, along with 40,000 half-length plaster figures, 250 monuments in praise of his achievements, 350 memorial halls and 3,500 "towers of eternal life."

Upon Kim Il Sung's death in 1994, twenty years of elaborate propaganda set the stage for his son Kim Jong Il to be proclaimed a god as well. The resulting Juche pantheon now provides for the worship of both the deceased Kim Il Sung—the title "Eternal President" whose spirit lives on to guide the Korean people—and the living Kim Jong Il. Pyongyang's propaganda demonstrates that, under the Juche religious system, Kim Jong Il is a coequal deity with his father:

> We regard the leader Kim Jong Il, who is identical to President Kim Il Sung in idea, leadership and virtue, as our mental support...We believe in the leader Kim Jong Il, who is the savior of nation and lodestar of national reunification (*Kuguk Jonson*[2]).

Kim Il Sung is also worshiped, in the sense that his spirit will live forever through the collective consciousness of the Party and masses.

The most recent development in Juche theology is the elevation in 1997 of Kim Jong Il's mother, Kim Jong Suk, to the status of a Juche goddess. Possibly because of the historical strength of Christianity in the North, Christian influence on Juche theology is reflected in Juche's triune godhead and surrogate "gospel." However, unlike the

---

2 Kuguk Jonson is an organ of the National Democratic Front of South Korea, an organization created by Pyongyang as a rallying point for pro-North activists in the South.

coequal Trinity of orthodox Christianity, Juche propaganda presents three separate gods with Kim Jong Suk in a supporting role to Kim Il Sung (the father) and Kim Jong Il (the son). The Juche idea has even latched onto the Christian idea of Holy Spirit fire: The "Tower of the Juche Idea" in Pyongyang is topped by a massive glass flame, lit in such a way as to appear to be eternally burning.

The Juche ideology dominates every aspect of life in North Korea: art, music, and literature all feed the people a constant stream of propaganda. Even children as young as two years of age are taught to sing hymns to the "Great Leader" and his "Dear Leader" son. From preschool through university, one-third of all teaching is aimed at strengthening the personality cult of the Kims.

North Korean masses march across the river from the Juche Tower.

VOM FIELD REPORT

The following report came from a VOM worker visiting northern China in 2005.

I am standing near the North Korean border beside a long-time VOM coworker who handles much of VOM's ministry inside North Korea. As he looks over the city, he is pointing just beyond the empty park and tells me, "See that open spot just beyond the park? A few months ago, they executed thirty people there."

"In public?" I ask.

"In public. They have music playing and drive through the streets so everyone in the city will come out to see what's going on. An officer comes forward who serves as judge and jury and sentences each one to death. Then they are lined up and shot." He voice trails off as he finishes telling me about the executions. I know he has more to say, but he remains quiet.

"Did you know any of them?" I ask.

"Yes, I knew eighteen of them. They were our workers."

I knew executions were not uncommon in North Korea, but I was shocked to find out they were promoted as a "festive occasion," executing people in front of men, women, and children.

"Did you see the video?" our coworker asks.

"What video?"

"The video of the public execution that was just secretly filmed."

"Are you kidding? There is a video of a public execution?" I am shocked. "What was the man's crime?"

"He was caught trying to escape. Generally the first time you are caught you go to labor camp for re-education for a few weeks or months. The second time the penalty is more severe—two to five years in a labor camp. The third time, you can be executed. This man was probably caught three times trying to escape."

FAMINE AND DEATH: 1995-2000

It is nearly impossible to overstate the desperation of North Korea's people during the terrible famine years. Refugees leaving the country testified that each morning during the famine, they would wake up and check on all of their neighbors to see who was still alive. As many of 5 million of North Korea's 24 million people may have died—an astonishing 21 percent of the population.

A government document showed the monthly death rates in one mining town. Between January 1995 and June 1998, 19 percent of the townspeople starved to death. Many more died in a cholera epidemic. One in five citizens fled the town seeking food elsewhere.

In the midst of such desperate suffering, despair led to unspeakable horrors. Entire families would eat poison in order to die quickly rather than slowly starve to death. Parents sometimes attempted to sell their own children. Some killed and ate their own infants. Those in North Korea today who did not participate in cannibalism during the famine at least know of someone who did.

In 1998, a U.N. study found that two-thirds of North Korean children suffered from stunted growth. Sixteen percent of children age six and under were "acutely malnourished." An average North Korean is 20 centimeters (almost 8 inches)

shorter and weighs half as much as an average South Korean.

An entire generation of North Korean children will never develop to their full physical or mental capabilities simply because they didn't have proper nutrition during the key formative years.

North Koreans with outside contacts sent desperate pleas for help. Many sent letters to China, then took long train rides to the Chinese border, desperately hoping for some form of assistance. More often than not, help never came. Authorities in Chinese border towns collected dozens of bodies each day—people who died waiting for help that didn't arrive. So many people were dying that North Korean authorities stopped trying to record the names.

The North Korean government blamed the famine on natural disasters and the attacks of "imperialist" outsiders bent on dominating the spirit of the Korean people. However, in reality, their own government policy was the chief culprit.

The Destructive Policy

Kim Il Sung's government added to the problem by conscripting the world's fifth largest standing army, and these men and women needed food. In the 1980s, he raised the mandatory military service requirement from seven to thirteen years.

When famine came in the mid 1990s, troops began dropping dead from hunger. To provide food for his army, Kim Jong Il sent the army to farms to commandeer the rice crop. Not only did Kim steal food from citizens, but he also prevented them from finding other ways of feeding themselves. Kim Il Sung found the people easier to control if they were more urban; therefore, North Korean policy encouraged people to live in the cities. But city dwellers were forbidden to grow food in gardens or anywhere else. Suburban peasants were allowed tiny garden plots but were not allowed to sell food in urban areas.

The entire population was dependent on a precarious government rationing system, a system that couldn't withstand anything less than maximum crop output. Spontaneous farmers' markets were shut down by force, and those peddling food were arrested. Some county officials even rejected outside aid for fear of being labeled a "traitor" by the government. Local officials found themselves caught between their starving popu-

North Korea's famine led to incredible desperation.

lation and the unreasonable expectations of the national government in Pyongyang.

In Musan, a town near the Chinese border, the Party secretary banned the black-market sale of rice. The people of the city threatened to rebel, fearing they would die if the secretary remained in power. Authorities placed the blame on an "anti-government organization" and arrested 200 people. Twelve were publicly executed. Refugees later said half of the city's 130,000 people either died or fled.

The world seemed uninterested in their desperation, yet the North Korean government tightly controlled news of the dire situation. One aid group that reported on the terrible conditions was promptly banned from working in the country.

In the harshest days of the famine, the government advocated the making of "substitute food," which included tree bark, leaves, or even sawdust. The following translation of a Korean television broadcast (picked up by the BBC in 1998) gives their incredible explanation of this situation:

> Despite the difficult food conditions due to the imperialists' maneuvers to isolate and crush the Democratic People's Republic of Korea and due to natural calamities for several years running, the Taedonggang Iron Daily Necessities plant is contributing to its employees' diets by pro-

ducing substitute food using acacia leaves and various other plants.

Rather than sitting around and complaining, we are dauntlessly producing and supplying substitute foods.

I think this method of making food can be done easily and everywhere without effort if one only toils persistently. The food situation could grow many times more difficult than it is now. Food could even run out completely in the future. Our working class is not one that would be shaken or would collapse even if such a situation occurs.

Among the worst affected parts of the population were prisoners. What had been labor camps became death camps. At a coal-mining work camp in Hoeryong near the Chinese border, one-third of the inmates died between 1991 and 1995. An escapee from a gold-mining camp in South Hamgyong province reported that 2,000 out of 7,000 to 8,000 prisoners had died in just two years. The deaths in the prisons began to affect the rest of the country, since much of the economy was dependent on the food and coal produced by prisoners.

By 1990, the public food distribution system had essentially ground to a halt. Amid such hopeless conditions, thousands risked death to flee across the border into China. North Koreans

talked about how "free" they felt once they were inside communist China.

But they were not free. Chinese authorities offered rewards to Chinese citizens who turned in fleeing North Koreans. China called the starving people "economic migrants" and denied them any right to seek political asylum. Chinese police along the border had quotas for the number of North Koreans they were to capture. If they failed to meet their quota, their pay was docked. Reliable sources say the Chinese even allowed North Korean agents to cross into Chinese territory to round up refugees and return them to North Korea. Those who were captured were treated like cattle. Often iron wire was run through their noses or even under their collarbones, and they were tied together and dragged away.

As such atrocities continued, the Chinese government assured the world that all those being repatriated were treated well. And the North Korean regime continued to spend lavishly. In 1998, at the height of the famine, the government imported $2.6 million worth of watches from Switzerland. The number of $1,000 Omega watches that were imported tripled in the next three years, to a total of $10 million in 2001.

Yet even in the midst of such dire circumstances, God was at work. The incomparable suffering produced by the famine created an incomparable opportunity for the gospel.

REVIVAL FIRE BURNS AGAIN: 2000-2006

As thousands of North Koreans were fleeing the hunger and desperation of their homeland, Christian ministries with a heart for North Korea saw an opportunity. While the borders of the country were still closed to outsiders, insiders were crossing into China every day and could be reached. The desperate physical hunger was making a way for the spiritual hunger to be quenched.

Interestingly, a move of God's Spirit seemed to be afoot, as many were called to minister for Him in the Hermit Kingdom. Many of those working to plant seeds of the gospel among North Koreans today were called by God at about the same time from various places on earth.

One worker, whom we'll call "Pastor Kim," lives in China but ministers regularly in North Korea. He shared with VOM how God called him into ministry to North Koreans:

> I watched as the dead bodies slowly floated down the river. They were mostly women and children. A Chinese soldier stood at the bank and, using a long wooden pole, guided the bodies away from the Chinese bank and back over to the North Korean shore. It was becoming a frequent occurrence. The next day a woman's body had washed up on my leased farmland that

borders the river. As I approached her, I noticed a hole in her stomach. A small fish was still inside eating at her flesh. It was then that the Lord spoke to me. And in that moment I knew what I had to do.

The work of "Pastor Kim" and others like him is producing an eternal harvest.

It is not safe for us to identify all the different ministry outreaches to North Koreans, but we can share a broad overview of work being done to see a vibrant, growing church rise up in that nation.

Outside Work

Today in China, Christians are ready and willing to take in fleeing North Koreans, offering them not only food and shelter, but also the Bread of Life and Living Water of the gospel message.

North Koreans know the risk for those in China who offer them aid—they know fines and arrests await all who are caught helping refugees. As they see the willing spirit of service and sacrifice, as well as the warm sense of peace in the lives of Christian workers, many are drawn to follow the Savior who called those workers there.

If any refugees choose to trust in Christ, they are offered a Bible and discipleship training in order to drive deep roots into His Word. Many of those who are discipled have a great desire to return to their country and share the gospel with their friends and families—those left behind to suffer under the oppressive regime.

There are other Christian works going on outside North Korea. The Voice of the Martyrs and our coworkers have launched tens of thousands of "Scripture balloons." Today we are using large balloons that can carry up to 10,000 gospel tracts which are released gradually over North Korea using a time-release mechanism. When the wind is right, the balloons are launched and carried over the border into North Korea.

"Scripture Balloons" can carry 10,000 gospel tracts.

Our contacts report that after some balloon launches, the North Korean army is mobilized to find and destroy all of the "imperialist propaganda," yet numerous North Koreans have said they first read the Good News of Jesus on "something like a trash bag."

There are also radio broadcasts proclaiming Jesus on the North Korean airwaves. The government tries to control every radio in the country, allowing them to be tuned only to propaganda-spouting "approved" stations. But radios can be modified, and black market units from China can be purchased that pick up the Christian signals.

Pray that these and other gospel "seeds" being sown into the hearts of North Koreans will fall on fertile soil.

Inside Work

We must be careful what we report of the ministry work going on inside North Korea. With Christians being executed routinely, it is a very dangerous place to minister.

There is, however, a growing church in North Korea, and Christians workers are seeing people come to know Christ and churches established.

One Christian worker has helped to establish a network of a hundred house churches and has personally delivered a Bible to each congregation. Such exciting growth, though, is not coming without cost. Getting Bibles into the country is one of the greatest needs, but being caught with one is a sure way to be imprisoned or executed.

A Christian leader reported that three workers in his group were executed in North Korea. Another eight workers were imprisoned.

In September 2007, the National Security Service held a press conference in Pyongyang to announce the arrest of "foreign spies" and "native citizens working for a foreign intelligence service." VOM sources say those arrested were not spies, as claimed by the government, but Christians. Nine Christians in North Korea suddenly disappeared during the summer of 2007; it is believed that those missing were arrested and accused of treason. It is not clear if they are still alive. Contacts familiar with the case believe they have been executed.

In another case, a Christian man named Son Jong Nam was arrested and sentenced in 2006 to be executed. The government said he had left the country illegally when he went to China and met with his brother, who escaped North Korea and now lives in South Korea. His brother encouraged Son Jong Nam to flee with him back to South Korea, but Son said that he could not leave as God had called him to minister in his homeland. Shortly after returning to North Korea, he was arrested. Most North Koreans who are caught after illegally visiting China are detained for a few months. Son Jong Nam's death sentence shows that his case is more about his faith in Christ and his ministry work than it is about his travels.

VOM sources reported that as of March 2007, Son Jong Nam was still alive in a prison in Pyongyang, awaiting execution. VOM launched an international campaign to raise awareness of his case. The North Korean government has yet to acknowledge Son's arrest, or even his existence.

Those working in such dangerous surroundings are careful not to compromise the believers. It is dangerous even to introduce a member of one house group to a member of another group. Despite the risks, there are networks of churches that are in operation. More people are coming to Christ, and churches are growing.

THE ROAD AHEAD:
PRAY FOR NORTH KOREA

After Kim Il Sung began to rule the nation, hundreds of churches in North Korea were destroyed and hundreds of thousands of Christians were martyred. The persecution was so extreme, many believed there were no survivors. It was thought by some that any remaining "Christians" must surely be puppets of the government, like the Bong-su and Chil-gol churches in Pyongyang. However, we now know beyond doubt of the continued existence of the true Church of Jesus Christ in North Korea. No matter what efforts the enemy makes to destroy it, God is greater and His Holy Spirit will guard and nurture His people. Not only are portions of the true Church still active, but they are also connected into larger geographic networks of believers. There is no stopping God. There is no way to cut off His Body.

From political and humanitarian viewpoints, the situation in North Korea is nothing short of desperate. An estimated 10 to 12 percent of the North Korean population has starved to death in less than a decade. Public executions, even for the smallest of crimes, are common. And it is not just the offender who is punished. The regime believes that to eradicate the opposition they must deal with three generations. Within the dozens of labor camps are prisoners of all ages, including young children. Hopelessness is epidemic, and most children have forgotten how to laugh or cry. They simply exist from one day to the next.

When VOM met with a Christian worker who travels regularly into North Korea and has an extensive network of contacts there, the message sent to American Christians was a very clear one: "*Tell the world!* Please tell the world about our brothers and sisters in North Korea." The impetus for this book is to fulfill her request: that the world may know the grave situation for believers and nonbelievers in North Korea.

Yet to the careful observer, there are signs of hope. VOM contacts report the regime's grip is weakening in some outlying areas of North Korea. The country's infrastructure is fraying, making it

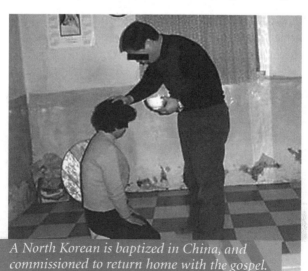

A North Korean is baptized in China, and commissioned to return home with the gospel.

more difficult for Kim Jong Il to maintain an iron-fisted grip on every person and inch of land.

There is also hope in the form of revival. Hundreds, maybe thousands, of North Koreans have escaped into China, heard the gospel and placed their trust in Jesus Christ. Many have traveled back to tell family and friends in the Hermit Kingdom. They know the risk. They know the penalty for following the One their government derides as "the God of heaven." And yet the message of hope burns so deeply in their hearts that they willingly take the risk to share the message.

Should they speak to you right now, the Christians in North Korea would have a simple request: Pray for us.

Will you fulfill their request? Will you pray for those who are suffering in political prisoner camps and for those being pressured to deny their faith in Christ? Will you pray for starving children who haven't yet heard the name of Jesus? Will you pray for young women who will flee this very night across the river into China, seeking food for their families or a better life for themselves? Will you pray for Christian workers planting the seeds of the gospel among the Juche-bound masses and for those living in poverty and desperation while their leaders live lives of pleasure and excess? Will you pray for the Lord of the harvest to send more workers into this ripe field?

Hear the North Korean Christians' plea: "Pray for us. Pray for us. *Pray for us.*"

FOR FURTHER READING

Following are some of the resources that served as source material for this book and for VOM workers researching the history of the church and persecution in North Korea.

Becker, Jasper. 2005. *Rogue Regime: Kim Jong Il and the Looming Threat of North Korea*. New York: Oxford University Press.

Belke, Thomas J. 1999. *Juche: A Christian Study of North Korea's State Religion*. Bartlesville, OK: Living Sacrifice Book Company.

Blair, William, and Bruce Hunt. 1977. *The Korean Pentecost and the Sufferings Which Followed*. Edinburgh, Scotland: The Banner of Truth Trust.

Lee, Soon Ok. 1999. *Eyes of the Tailless Animals: Prison Memoirs of a North Korean Woman*. Bartlesville, OK: Living Sacrifice Book Company.

Moffett, Samuel Hugh. 1962. *The Christians of Korea*. Cinncinnati, OH: Friendship Press, Inc.

Owens, Donald D. 1977. Revival Fires in Korea. Kansas City, MO: Nazarene Publishing House.

Online Resources
Official North Korean Government website: www.korea-dpr.com

World Factbook: https://www.cia.gov/library/publications/the-world-factbook/index.html